E K MAWLONG

A POLITICAL BIOGRAPHY

Ferdinand Banshanlang Lyngdoh

Vitasta

Published by
Renu Kaul Verma
Vitasta Publishing Pvt Ltd
2/15, Ansari Road, Daryaganj
New Delhi - 110 002
info@vitastapublishing.com

ISBN 978-93-90961-04-7

First Edition 2022

MRP ₹595

Edited by Manjula Lal
Cover and layout by Somesh Kumar Mishra
Printed at Chaman Enterprises, New Delhi

CONTENTS

For my father and mother, who instilled in
me the patience to endure.

Thank you for all your sacrifices.

FERDINAND LYNGDOH MAWPHLANG
31 August 1984-2 October 2021

TAKE ME HOME...

When 'Ma'am' Renu K. Verma of Vitasta Publishing Pvt. Ltd, New Delhi, suggested that I should write a "tribute" to my dear younger brother, Ferdinand aka Ferdy aka Nan, to be incorporated in this book, I began to ponder – from where should I start? Should I just narrate his CV? Should I share simple memories? Should I…Should I…Should I…? For a journalist, it is not so difficult to jot down a piece based on the facts at hand. For a brother, it is.

Well, I don't know what you would like to call this – a tribute, an ode to a departed brother, heartfelt tears for a soul gone too soon, a goodbye note, a thank you. It is not easy to write about Ferdy. He wore many hats simultaneously. From a scholar to a brilliant teacher, a caring son, a reliable brother, a doting husband and father, a great friend, no matter what the weather was like, a passionate musician, a zealous sportsman, a not-too-bad cook, and more. He was loved for different reasons by different people.

In his short but eventful life spread across the compounds of our home at Lumsohphoh, Lower Mawprem, to his first school at Persara, and to the hallowed halls of St. Edmund's, Shillong, to the sprawling fields of Assam Rifles Public School at Laitkor and the inspirational buildings of St. Edmund's College and the enormous land housing the North Eastern Hill University, to the mammoth compound of the College of Community Science, Sangsanggre at Tura, and to his adorable daughter and wife's home at Matchakholggre at New Tura – Ferdy had undoubtedly lived his life to the brim. Short but sweet although he had his share of bitter-sweet moments like all of us mortals.

From August 31, 1984, the day he came into this world, till October 2, 2021, the day he completed his earthly journey, I firmly believe that there was never a dull moment in Ferdy's life. From childhood to fatherhood, Ferdy wasn't someone who would just disappear into the crowd and be forgotten. That spark in him is what radiates till this moment and makes him stand apart, although his humility would never make him notice the difference he emanated and the difference he made.

We will continue to mourn his demise. We still grieve. We feel the heartwrenching pain. We still have tears. But when the "good old days" make a comeback, subconsciously or otherwise, we smile. We want to remember him that way – a person who brought smiles to many no matter what the odds were. Yes, we will celebrate his life, too, for being the good soul that he was.

In the cold winter of Shillong, I am reminded of two autumns, separated by 13 years and 16 days, and which have not been kind to us.

Being a passionate musician, I guess he must have played or sung or hummed John Denver's "Take Me Home, Country Roads" as he zoomed from the hills of Tura to the hills of Shillong – about 321 km or so – via Guwahati, the mother of all cities in our Northeast, on the morning of October 2, 2021.

It was a Saturday, and the world was observing Gandhi Jayanti. The Mahatma, of whom the great scientist, Albert Einstein, had said: "Generations to come will scarce believe that such a one as this ever in flesh and blood walked upon this earth."

But as the world paid tributes to the Mahatma, we, as a family, were shattered upon learning about the tragic fate, which befell on our dear Ferdinand.

Many of us at home, did not know that he was travelling from Tura to Shillong alone in his Mahindra Bolero vehicle, which he purchased from Shillong in August 2020. But what we did know later was that on that fateful day, at around 9:30 in the morning, he informed my elder sister, Damaphi, that he was on his way home. His intention of coming home was to get his vehicle serviced. And he had not been home for quite a few months. But, yes, the country roads did take him home, to the place he belonged, but painfully, not the way anyone had fathomed.

I was in bed when I received a video of a Bolero vehicle up in flames along National Highway-6 on the Guwahati-Shillong Road. As a journalist, the first thought that came to my mind was to ask the sender where the location of the accident was. But before I could get clear answers, Damaphi came rushing to my room to inquire about the burning vehicle. I was frightened when she informed me that even our Ferdy was on his way home driving his Bolero. "Could this be HIS Bolero?" I pondered, fervently hoping and praying that it wasn't HIS.

But it did not take time to get confirmation that it was indeed Ferdy's vehicle. While watching the video, I could see the door from the driver's seat open. "Maybe he got out in time. Maybe passersby took him to the hospital. Maybe he struggled and could finally get himself out of the vehicle." The maybes were making me hopeful. Ferdy was fit as a fiddle with quick reflexes. However, that wasn't to be on the Mahatma's birth anniversary. He died inside the vehicle, which was neatly parked in a desolate spot along the highway at Umsalem village under the Umsning police outpost in Ri Bhoi district.

Numbed. Shattered. Shocked. No real adjectives to describe what everyone was going through that day, and the days that followed, and till this very moment. Mother, whom he would always inform before making a trip home, was inconsolable.

Nobody can fathom the immense pain caused by the loss of a child more than a mother. Just like Mother's love, her pain is indescribable. Only she knows. To this day, she grapples with the pain. Her eyes say it all.

Accompanied by our eldest brother, George, to whom Ferdy was strong support, the mortal remains of the young father and husband, brilliant teacher, proficient writer, a friend of everyone, an enemy of the wrongdoers, fearless human, risk-taker, passionate musician, sporting sportsman, the leader in every field and a hero who never yielded (to paraphrase our school anthem), made its way home to Lumsohphoh, Lower Mawprem at around 9:30 PM. He was home – the home which he grew up in, and where we shared joy, love, tears.

Scores of mourners from far and near came to bid farewell to our Ferdy. From the high and mighty to the hoi polloi, which depicted Ferdy's character – equally at ease to sit around with those in tuxedoes or with those who were economically disadvantaged. Those who knew him and even those who didn't come. Many were in tears of utter disbelief, shock, agony and pain. They felt our pain. They shared our grief. October 3, 2021, was Ferdy's final journey. His mortal remains were taken to the Catholic Cemetery at Upper Mawprem. The grave was not too distant away from where we had placed the mortal remains of our late Father in the autumn of 2008.

Among the many memories, people, and work

he left behind, Ferdy was fortunate to have seen the final draft of the fruit of his labour and love – this book, the biography of our late Father. George informed us that around 10:58 AM on that tragic day, he received the final draft on WhatsApp. Ferdy had forwarded it to George after the publisher had sent him. From the word go, Ferdy had slogged for this book. It was his baby. It is his accomplishment. It embodies his sweat. How much we wish that Ferdy was here to see this book in print and proudly hold it up for everyone to see.

But without our two pillars of strength – Priya Talwar and Renu – it would have been impossible to take this book to its logical conclusion. Before Ferdy's demise, none of us knew much about the book – maybe he had purposely kept it away from everyone until 'D-Day'. However, Priya was the constant in this journey. In November, George, our dear friend Fernandez and I took a flight to Delhi to meet Priya and Renu to discuss the book. They all said it was ready; just give them the word and the printing machine would roll. Behold, here it is! Thank you, Priya and Renu. We owe you.

We believe Ferdy is in a better world with our Father. The duo must be smiling down as they witness the launch of this book. They are now stars in heaven after having completed their earthly journey. The country roads have taken them to a better world, a better place, and their heavenly home.

—Andrew W Lyngdoh

PUBLISHER'S NOTE

It is usual to see authors get impatient about their books, not wanting to wait for the production process to complete, but not Ferdinand. He was more than happy to let his ready-to print-book wait to coincide with the 50th year celebration of Meghalaya in 2022. Such was his devotion to his motherland. Always polite, patient, and committed, Ferdy was just the kind of author any publisher would love to have.

A day before his passing, he wanted a picture of his father replaced in the book that he had penned down so passionately. We sent the file back to him hoping he would have the time to go through it during the weekend. Unfortunately, fate had willed otherwise.

Manjula Lal, who edited his book, shared a newspaper clipping that broke the tragic news. We were shell-shocked. Such a sad fate for someone so young. It seems unbelievable that he is no longer with us. We cannot even imagine the grief of his family. We hope they find peace and solace in his memories.

As his publisher, we will make sure that the book's journey continues as per his wishes, but alas he will not be there in the physical form to witness his dream come true.

IN MEMORIAM

Ferdy was a special author not merely because he was the first author I signed up with as a literary agent but also because we worked together for almost 2 years and the one thing that struck about him was how he never behaved as if he was entitled to anything.

You are missed Ferdy, very much.

I did not get to say this but I adored you, for your warmth and honesty.

Lots of love,

—Priya Talwar
Literary Agent

FOREWORD

EK Mawlong (1946-2008), political firebrand, architect of the United Democratic Party, former Chief Minister and Speaker of the Meghalaya Legislative Assembly, has many feathers to his cap, many titles worth mentioning.

What most people are unaware of was the friendship Mawlong shared with my father, Late Purno A Sangma.

Aside from their political rivalry, what was admirable was their mutual respect for one another. They shared a meaningful friendship from their college days when my father, an orphan boy, was taken under the care of the Jesuit brothers. From sharing a room in St Stephen's Hall to being college mates at St Anthony's College, their bond grew stronger over the years. It was obvious that the credit to their long, shared friendship was a result of their shared vision, and love for Meghalaya.

They both worked for the betterment of

Meghalaya, fervent in their beliefs, equally persistent and adamant in their opinions. In the Legislative Assembly, they debated head-on, both headstrong, both passionate, but behind the table tapping and differences, their friendship remained unaffected.

I believe their differences inspired them in their pursuits; it fueled their ambitions for separate political parties. I believe they inspired each other immensely as mentors, friends, rivals-unflinching in their common vision for Meghalaya.

Conrad K Sangma
Chief Minister, Meghalaya

ACKNOWLEDGEMENTS

This biography is a protracted effort which wouldn't have been possible without the generous contribution of a host of relatives, friends, and political leaders.

I am thankful to Conrad K Sangma, Chief Minister of Meghalaya for the Foreword, and to the political leaders of our state—SD Khongwir, Beningstand G Momin, Bindo M Lanong, Luderberg Ch Momin, H Donkupar Roy Lyngdoh, Process T Sawkmie, (L) Hispreaching Son Shylla, and a host of other political leaders for their invaluable and forthright observations.

I am obliged to Dr Andrew Simons, Commissioner and Secretary of the Meghalaya Legislative Assembly, for granting access to all the published and unpublished proceedings of the House, and to all the staff of the Library of the Meghalaya Legislative Assembly for their assistance. I also thank the authorities of the Khasi

Hills Autonomous District Council (KHADC) for providing hardcopies of the proceedings of the relevant years.

To my friend Dr Dhiraj Borkotoky, who is now at Royal Global University, Guwahati, and Emdordini Thangkhiew, Joplin Hek, and their colleagues at the International Centre for North-East Studies, Synod College, Shillong, I am much obliged for their resourcefulness and dedicated research work.

My gratitude especially to all my paternal relations of Mawmih village.

To Fr John Madur, Fr Sylvanus Nongkynrih, Sr Anita Wahlang, Babu Dwikshon Kharkongor, Prof Helen Giri Syiem, Prof Chosterfield Khongwir, and KM Warjri, who sat through endless cups of tea scouring numerous memorable incidences. I thank Billy Domes, EL Lyttan, PR Hinge, Aldous Mawlong, EM Jose, and many of my father's friends who sent write-ups as contributions to the book.

I am indebted to Professor Susmita Sengupta of the Department of Political Science, North-Eastern Hill University, Shillong, for her conscientious review of the portions on the political history of Meghalaya.

To my uncle Late Shanbok Lyngdoh Mawphlang, I owe my thanks for his meticulous dedication in retrieving the records particularly related to the years 2000 and 2001.

For their joviality and expediency, I thank my

friends Raymond Kharmujai, Rining Lyngdoh Mawphlang, Bishar L Dhar, Dester Hinge, Biwot Lanong, John Henry Lyngdoh Mawphlang, Wankerlang Nongbet, Benjamin Neuman Syiem, John Thounaojam, Vikas Chongtham, Jiko Kharbuki, Yoihenba Chongtham, and Ritu G Momin.

Thank you, Chetan Mahajan and Namrata Madhira of the Himalayan Writing Retreat for your guidance and much-needed inspiration.

Priya Talwar of Editor's Atelier, for agreeing to edit the book as well as represent me as a literary agent, hand-holding me at every step of this wonderful experience. Thank you, Priya.

Publishing a book is a slow process and a labour of love. I owe gratitude to Renu Kaul Verma of Vitasta for believing in this invaluable project. A special thanks to Alisha Verma and Manjula Lal for their editorial inputs.

Lastly, I will forever be in gratitude to my mother and siblings, and the people of Umroi constituency—the equally steadfast pillars of my beloved father, without whom this book wouldn't have found a place in this world.

INTRODUCTION

This biography was conceptualised in the year 2009, months after Evansius Kek Mawlong, the seventh Chief Minister of Meghalaya passed away at a relatively young age of 62. A serious attempt was made only eight years later in 2017, when the International Centre for North-East Studies, Synod College, Shillong was asked to conduct an in-depth research on his political career. The team led by Dr Dhiraj Borkotoky exhibited immense academic prowess and submitted a comprehensive report after a year and a half of diligent work. However, documenting the incredible rise of Evansius Kek Mawlong from a cowherd in a nondescript village in East Khasi Hills to the highest executive office in the state simply needed more work. This is when I took over the endeavour to complete the biography.

In 2017, I was working as an Assistant Professor in the College of Community Science, Central Agricultural University, Tura and was able to afford only a few hours daily. It was not until April 2020, three years later, that I could give the biography the attention it deserved.

During the national lockdown imposed due to COVID-19, I was able to find the time to write about my father's enormous contribution to the state of Meghalaya in general, and his beloved people of Umroi constituency in particular.

After the lockdown eased, I visited Umroi to meet the older folks who were politically active from the 1970s till the 1990s. Most of them shared a common view about 'Bah Heh Kek', as his peers called him. They remembered him as the cheerful man in a white Ambassador car, wearing a straw hat on his head, waving at them. Mawlong, they told me, would shake hands with lay people with the same respect as dignitaries. He would call out children to line up for sweets and tell them stories. They told me that once upon a time, Umroi was a *shrah*[1] because of the impenetrable vegetation in most of the villages and that it was Mawlong who was the pioneer in executing Government schemes and bringing immense growth and development to Umroi. They also told me about his frequent visits to the constituency, not just before elections. Yet, they also told me that they regretted his overconfidence, which was partly the reason he lost the 2003 elections.

1 Inaccessible place

What struck me most was that they wished he should have been a priest instead of a politician. Ultimately, Mawlong was their Pa Trai,[2] the biological father of Umroi, who is known to have strived tirelessly to bring positive changes in his near four-decade career in politics. Even when he was physically tired and ill, he refused to stop doing what he loved the most–to selflessly serve the people.

The biography aims to capture his life from his boyhood days till the day he passed away on 18 October 2008. A considerable portion of it is dedicated to his contribution to the welfare of Umroi and its people. Apart from briefly touching upon the political history of Meghalaya from the 1970s to the 1990s, it also addresses the socio-economic issues he raised in the Assembly as an outspoken member of the opposition, his contribution as Speaker of the House, and his work as Chief Minister of the state. Primary sources of the biography include personal newspaper cuttings, digitised assembly proceedings, home videos of his election rallies, interviews with his friends and political foes, and write-ups from contemporaries. A major limitation was that some information related to his early life could not be ascertained.

Although ambition helped him reach the highest echelons of power, it was not without facing a downside. In 2001, Mawlong was falsely

2 Taken from a song sung by villagers of Ïapngar at a 1998 election rally at Ïew Umroi

accused of corruption in what is now known as the infamous Kolkata Meghalaya House deal. After a tiresome fight against the injustice for almost seven years, the High Court of Guwahati acquitted him ten months before he passed away. Though all paths of glory lead to the grave, what eventually matters is exoneration from injustice. Despite the political duplicity, his faith was steadfast, and ultimately, justice didn't forsake him.

Politics is rife with opportunists, and Meghalaya has witnessed the questionable acts of many a political turncoat. The regional parties in the state have had to confront such adversities on multiple occasions. And the drama of their coming together and breaking away has been played out several times in the five decades since the formation of the state. As a regionalist, Mawlong tried to bring about a change in such behaviour, projecting the regional parties as viable alternatives to the national ones.

However, the question remains: Did he succeed? I hope that readers are able to arrive at an understanding after reading the biography. The lesson I wish readers to derive from EK Mawlong's story, like I did, is that just like in love and war, everything is fair in politics. It is a complex mandala which the virtuous consider superfluous and the faint-hearted, brutish.

A KHASI FAMILY

THE WARM October sun eased the 16-degree chill of the Mawmih air. Two men and a woman burst into peals of laughter as they sat in a traditional kitchen, with smoke rising from their local tobacco joint. Siblings Isidora Jweit (80) and Heston (76), along with their nephew Sne (78), were talking about their beloved brother, Evansius Kek Mawlong, who had passed away ten years ago. Lud, as Isidora was fondly called at home, was telling them how her younger brother would occasionally get angry with his nephews and nieces whenever they were impish. Holding a stick in his hand, a plump Mawlong, also the eldest among the six brothers, would blurt out imaginary threats of whacking them black and blue.

The ancestral home at Mawmih village was the meeting place for most important family matters. On that chilly October afternoon in 2018, the trio wanted to pray together on Mawlong's tenth death anniversary.

In the Khasi community, it is a common sight to see family members huddled around the hearth, sharing stories of the previous generations.[1] In Mawmih, they lived in a sizeable house of wood and tin and a fireplace would keep them warm through the cold year. The family owned a Ïing Basa,[2] and the smallest of pleasures meant cooking together. While their mother would brew *kyiad*[3] for the visiting men, little Lud would 'playfully dig her fingers into sacks of uncooked rice and Bah[4] would pull and roll dry yeast between his fingers'. The resting house had a huge chimney that stood like the Babel Tower puffing an endless procession of smoke.

Isidora says that her six brothers were always running like roes on the hills, pulling a cow here and a goat there. 'Bah was the only one among the boys who was really interested in going to school,' she says.

Evansius Kek Mawlong was born on 1 February 1946 to Yiem Mawlong and Sajerson Thangkhiew in Mawmih village in the East Khasi district of Meghalaya. The Khasi couple bore seven children (Jnger, Isidora, Evansius, Haron, Heston, Eshon,

1 Oral narrations and storytelling are important aspects of Khasi culture as most of its literature is unwritten

2 Traditional rest house

3 Local brew

4 Eldest son of the family/formal way of addressing a man; here, referring to Evansius

and Kestian). When Evansius was about eight years old, Sajerson Thangkhiew, a native of Mawmih, passed away.[5] Yiem Mawlong remarried in the late 1950s and bore two children, Ephraiñ and Idimai, with Nokim Marbaniang.

Among the three main indigenous tribes of Meghalaya, including Jaiñtia and Garo, the Khasi tribe is the most populous. All tribes follow the matrilineal customary practice of tracing their lineage from women. Ancestral property is also traditionally passed on from the parents to the youngest daughter of the family.

Another integral aspect of the Khasi identity is the *kur* or clan,[6] a kinship group, where the group bears a common surname. Most of the clans trace their roots from their respective great-grandmothers, *ki ïawbei tynrai*. Descendants of the same ancestress of the clans, *ka ïawbei tynrai,* belong to the same clan and call themselves *ki shi kur*.

It is believed that the Mawlong clan members have their antecedents in the Nongbah-Nartiang area of Jaiñtia Hills of the state. The Mawlong clan traces its origins to a woman who was originally from Nongbah-Nartiang. Many believe that the woman was falsely accused of killing an infant.

5 There is no clear record of the circumstances leading to his death

6 The word 'clan' or 'kur' refers to all groups of people, both male and female, who descend from the first mother or clan ancestress of the family line known as 'Ka Ïawbei'. While relatives from the maternal clan are called ki kur, relatives from the father's clan are called ki kha.

When faced with a mob wanting to avenge the murder of an innocent child, she fled through thick forests. On hearing approaching footsteps or impending danger, she hid behind large plantain leaves. She kept walking until she reached a village in the West Khasi Hills. The woman later made the village, Mairang, her home and stayed behind a huge boulder. The clan title Mawlong[7] was conferred after the large boulder where she found shelter. Gradually, descendants proliferated all over the Khasi Hills, but remained largely concentrated in Mairang and the Diengïei areas of Krang, Kreit, and Mawmih.

The progenitors of the Mawlong clan in Mawmih were hard-working individuals who tilled the earth as farmers and engaged in other economic activities to survive. The entire Mawlong clan of Mawmih and its surrounding villages have plenty of *Ki Ri-Kynti*.[8] Such property is not owned by one individual or a particular family. Instead, members from a common clan ancestor are equal shareholders of land and its resources. The clan members, led by the uncles, decide upon the utilisation of valuable resources such as land.

As the youngest daughter, Yiem Mawlong inherited a large Assam-type house in the centre of Mawmih village. Yiem was in charge of *ka ïing basa,* a traditional rest house which provided shelter

7 Large stone
8 Property owned by a clan

to travellers in search of better economic means and visiting relatives. She also ran a brewery and owned plenty of livestock. Her children, including Evansius Kek, spent most of their childhood in Mawmih. However, much of their later teenage and adult years were spent in Ñiangdai and Umjymphod.

The hilly terrain of Mawmih was unsuitable for large-scale agriculture. Yiem and her siblings inherited land in Ñiangdai, Umtring, and Umjymphod villages, and decided to harvest paddy to support the family. Yiem also invested in a large dairy farm. Rice cultivated in the plainer and more fertile areas of the villages would then be transported on horseback to Mawmih. They also set up a local brewery in the enclosure of her house, using rice from the fields to brew the alcohol. While most of it was sold locally, some was traded to neighbouring villages.

Yiem saved most of her earnings in sacks made out of a tough cloth material, locally called *muna*. Known for her generosity, especially towards orphans, she nurtured many relatives' children who weren't as financially stable or those whose parents had passed away. Evansius Kek Mawlong's first cousin, Shran Mawlong, and another lifelong friend in his later years, Arbat Kurbah, were brought up by Yiem Mawlong.

Although Khasi society accords centrality to women, owing to its matrilineal practice and inheritance structure, the importance of men

as sons, brothers, fathers, and particularly as uncles, cannot be ignored. Being the first born son or *u khun phrang sngi*, Mawlong felt a certain responsibility and also received enormous respect from his siblings and relatives.

THE EARLY YEARS

IN 1953, Mawlong completed his primary education from the Roman Catholic Lower Primary School, started by Catholic priests as part of their missionary work. Since the school in Kreit village, the only school in fact, provided education till primary school, his parents and teachers wished to send the bright student to a better school, which meant moving out of the village. This was the primary reason he went to Don Bosco Technical School in Shillong. There are, however, two accounts of how Mawlong landed in the state capital Shillong from Mawmih.

On an Easter Monday in 1953, a picnic was organised by Rev Fr Virgilius Albeira, a Salesian priest and then Rector of Don Bosco Technical School, Shillong, for the students who did well in catechism.[9] Dr S Loniak Marbaniang, one

---

9 Moral and spiritual teaching imparted particularly in Catholic missionary schools

of the students who had excelled in the subject, was part of the picnic and recollected the events of the day. A group of 10 or 15 boys led by Fr Albeira drove two hours from Shillong to Mawmih village, popular for a clear water stream. When they reached, a group of local boys looked at the uniformed students with wonder but soon enough started playing around the jeep in which the school students had come. Fr Albeira, who was fond of young children, encouraged the two groups to play together. Although initially reluctant, the school students slowly inched closer to share their food.

Loniak Marbaniang had noticed a boy smiling shyly among his new friends when the Italian priest turned to the village boys and said, 'Khynnah,[10] Look at that jeep. All these hostel boys have sat in that vehicle and are celebrating because they have all done well in school. Don't you want to sit in it?' If they attended school and studied well, he told them, he would give them a ride in the jeep. Marbaniang saw that only one boy was listening patiently to Father. On noticing the young Mawlong, Father walked towards him and asked him if he would like to visit Shillong. 'If you study there, I think you will do very well. If you work hard, you will achieve a lot.'

It was a year after this incident that Mawlong arrived in Don Bosco as a hosteller.

10 Children

There is another account of what may have encouraged him to study in Shillong. In his early years, two teachers left a huge impression on Mawlong. The first one was Renatus Ebit Lamare, one of his teachers in the primary school at Kreit. He was from Laitumkhrah locality in Shillong, and after marrying a cousin of Mawlong, had settled at Mawmih. The other prominent teacher was Babu[11] Marius Dliton Shadap, who was from Mawkyrdep, a village in the vicinity of Umroi. Before he was transferred to Kriet, he was a teacher in the mission school in Umroi. Lamare and Shadap were passionate about their work but equally concerned about discipline. They were known for pulling children by their ears if they missed school. Lamare's daughter, Hilda Mawlong, who was seven years younger than Evansius Kek Mawlong, says that both the teachers encouraged him to study in Shillong as they must have seen his intelligence and sincerity. He would later even guide his niece when she was preparing for her matriculation.

In the late 1950s, when the rest house at Mawmih had become popular, an unforeseen event changed everything for the family. One morning, Yiem Mawlong woke up to see that the group of men who had arrived the night before had disappeared. They had also stolen the *muna*, which contained all her earnings from the produce

11 Teacher

she sold, including milk, rice and brew. There were many such bags stacked in the cupboards of the house and the robbers managed to steal most of them. From that point, the financial position of Mawlong's family changed drastically. Heston Mawlong, called Deng by his siblings, remembers how everything had to be rebuilt from scratch.

> Bah had already left for Shillong. At the house in Ñiangdai village, mother set up another brewery and a small piggery too. There were still plenty of *khuti*[12] of cows, and she leased them to Nepali men. The milk produced by us and the Nepalis in those days was of such excellent quality that traders from Shillong would drive in their Willys Jeeps all the way to Mawlyndep village, which was the meeting point.

In the days prior to the theft, Yiem employed a considerable number of helpers to work mainly in the brewery. The sudden shortfall in resources compelled Yiem to relieve most of them. Although she gradually reinvigorated her financial needs, restarting life wasn't easy. Many years later, Mawlong confided to his friends that at times they had to survive only on boiled potatoes. The sudden change in fortune for the family and the abject poverty of most of the people of Mawmih perhaps stirred in the young Mawlong a desire to excel in

12 Animal shed

education and empower himself.

Mawlong left home for studies, but his siblings Deng and Lud say that he did not stop visiting home, even when he was away for college and work thereafter. In fact, he would walk almost 5-6 hours from Shillong through Mawlai along *Ka Surok Rim*[13] to reach Nongpathaw, a village near Mawmih, as hardly anyone owned a vehicle. The moment he'd enter, he would always hum a tune, call his sister Isidora, and head straight to the fireplace in the kitchen to be of some help.

The robbery had forced the family to rely on limited means, including the reaped crop from the fields. The young Mawlong saw less of his mother as travelling to the city became an expensive affair. However, it is likely that the effect of this event left the strongest influence on Mawlong, believe his siblings.

13 An old road that connected Shillong to the Diengïei area

THE FORMATIVE YEARS

AT DON Bosco Technical School, Mawlong was known as a bright, helpful and diligent student. Billy P Domes, who studied in the same school got to know him in 1953 or 1954, later worked for the Government and became a journalist after retirement. Until about two decades ago, Domes says that there were two categories of pupils: those who learnt trades as artisans, and those like Mawlong who pursued only academics. Since Domes was older and ahead of Mawlong in class by 3-4 years, he got to know him well only years later. In a note addressed to the family, Domes wrote:

> Under normal circumstances, my recollection of Bah Kek should have been at most sketchy. But this was not so. During my remaining years in school, from 1955 when I left Don Bosco, to 1961 when I passed my matriculation, I would off and on get news about Bah Kek, who unlike many of us who stagnated in the still waters

> of mediocrity, was churning the waters to make waves through his achievements in studies.

On 14 December 1960, the young Mawlong received two honours in Don Bosco Technical School. He was awarded the first position in catechism in the school and also felicitated as the Best Boy of the school.

Another batchmate from Don Bosco, Arhiwot Rymbai, who is a retired Government employee, remembers how Mawlong would tutor him in his free time.

> Whenever I needed help in studies especially in the higher classes, Bah Kek would always patiently explain topics that he understood better. He was exceptional in mathematics.

He adds that Mawlong's handwriting was as good as that of a trained calligrapher. Rymbai describes Mawlong as a gentle boy who hardly ever lost his cool over anything, a friend with whom he could share stories of triumph or struggle, as well as things even when they did not have enough.

> Though he was silent and kept things within himself, he would confide to me about the insecurity of being the eldest son in an extensive family. He was often perturbed, thinking particularly of his mother's struggles who worked hard in the fields, juggling the role of a mother and provider. No matter how much he must

> have struggled within, he never let that show on his face or affect his studies.

Before the winter vacation, Mawlong would ask Rymbai to come to his village just to show how to milk a cow or remove the rice from its stalk but Rymbai never visited because of the distance. When they reached Class 10, Mawlong left the hostel and appeared for matriculation as a day scholar.

Yiem decided that her son should move out of the boarding house. A village boy who had no immediate relatives in the city, Mawlong got lucky when Babu Sosto Manik Syiem took him under his tutelage in 1962. Babu Syiem was a respectable personality known to Yiem Mawlong.

Babu Sosto Manik Syiem was a well-known teacher of Mawkhar Christian School, who owned plots of land in the villages of Umpanai and Ñiangdai and stayed in Mawkhar locality in Shillong. During his trips to his private property in the village, he befriended Mawlong's parents, who worked on their own paddy field and dairy farm. One thing led to another and the two families became close.

Since Babu Syiem was a reputed teacher, the young Mawlong's family requested him to be their son's benefactor and guide, particularly before the matriculation examination. Babu Syiem found a place for the adolescent boy in his sister's enormous house at Mawkhar locality. This way, Mawlong could visit the teacher whenever needed.

Despite having children, Babu Syiem's brother-in-law provided shelter for other boys and girls from distant villages. One of his daughters, Helen Giri Syiem, became thick friends with the young Mawlong.

> The first time I saw Evan–I always called him Evan because I did not like the name Kek–was when he was still in school. I was studying in Lady Keane College in BA, third year. The state of Meghalaya didn't exist, and all schools and colleges were still under Guwahati or Calcutta University.

In fact, when Babu Syiem took Mawlong to Helen's father, he embraced him like a son. One day, the young Mawlong was standing in the front yard of Helen's house when she called his name. He was standing outside the house in a white shirt, loose trousers, and spectacles. Helen shouted at him, '*Ei! I khynnah aiu ine*?' (Hey! Who is this boy?) When he tried to run away, she asked him his name and what he was doing there. An intimidated Mawlong did not say anything until Helen's father clarified that it was Babu Syiem who brought him there. Helen, who later became a professor of history in the North-Eastern Hill University and is also a renowned folk musician and music instructor, recalls the incident.

> I took him aside and asked, 'What is your name?' He answered meekly, 'Kek...Kek Mawlong.'

> 'Kek? What? Kek?' I said. 'What kind of name is that? Don't you have a better name?'

'Evan...Evansius Kek Mawlong,' he replied shyly. 'Hmm...From today onwards, I will call you Evan. And don't let anyone call you by that horrible name.'

Helen's father provided a room to Mawlong, where he stayed and studied for his matriculation. Many times, she reminded him in a serious tone that he should work harder. 'Get up early, Evan,' Helen would say. 'Set your alarm clock before the rooster crows. We should compete with the better students always.' A few days later, the diligent Mawlong approached Helen with the alarm clock in hand. 'Kong, please teach me how to set this alarm. I want it to ring at four tomorrow morning,' the boy said eagerly.

The Seng Khasi[14] Hall in Mawkhar was close to Helen's ancestral house. They would spend hours watching men and women dance to the beat of the *ksing*[15] and the wails of the *tangmuri*[16] during the Shad Suk Mynsiem[17] festival. Evan would join Helen and her siblings to watch the dancing

---

14 An indigenous Khasi group founded on November 23, 1899

15 Traditional Khasi cylindrical drum

16 Traditional Khasi wind instrument

17 Shad Suk Mynsiem literally means to dance heartily or to dance with a joyful heart; it is an annual traditional dance festival organised by the Seng Khasi in April to commemorate the season of spring.

men and maidens. Helen would 'drag' him to the market, 'thrusting one enormous aluminium bowl into his hands' before they would 'run to buy fish.' For Helen, Mawlong was like a 'younger sibling' whom she could 'playfully bully around'.

Helen felt that he spoke quite softly, much like his mother, and started encouraging him to speak louder. 'Later, when he moved on to do wonderful things in life, he perhaps gained confidence with the exposure he got or the company he kept. But the one thing that never died in him was that inimitable village-boy simplicity.'

In 1963, Mawlong completed his matriculation with first division and joined St Anthony's College, Shillong to pursue his Pre-University (PU) in the science stream. Two years after completing it with a second division, he reluctantly enrolled for the Bachelor of Science programme in the same college since he wanted to study English as his major subject. The Principal of the time, Fr Joseph Arokiaswamy and Hostel Warden Fr NJ Kenny felt Mawlong had a better aptitude for science and advised him that studying science will help gain employment eventually.

Mawlong initially stayed at the Parish Compound, Laitumkhrah with the family of his primary school teacher, Renetus Ebit Lamare. During his time at Laitumkhrah, he became close friends with Dr S Loniak Marbaniang. The two had first met fleetingly during the 1953 Easter picnic

and later in school. Dr Marbaniang, who retired as Professor of Mathematics at the North-Eastern Hill University, Shillong and is also a former Legislator and Minister of Education, says that their friendship began when Mawlong was in college. Marbaniang belonged to Lyngkhoi, a place near Mawphlang in the East Khasi Hills district and later shifted to Laitumkhrah. 'Bah Kek was regular in attending Sunday Mass at the Cathedral, and the after-church conversations during our walks back home was how we got to know one another well.' Later, they worked together in the church activities as members of the Catholic Managing Committee (CMC) of Laitumkhrah Block A locality. Since Marbaniang was the President and Mawlong the Secretary, they organised prayer meetings and house visits to raise funds for the needy. They also helped the church authorities in organising various programmes, including the annual Eucharistic procession in Laitumkhrah, the largest congregation of Catholics in the state. Working together for social initiatives brought them closer to each other and also to the church's clergy.

When the family he was staying with shifted to a rented house in Mawkhar, Mawlong got a seat in the Stephen Hall Hostel for Boys at Bomfyle Road, a hostel only for college students. His room-mates were Arhiwot Rymbai and Purno Agitok Sangma, both of whom became close friends later, especially Sangma, who also embarked upon a career in politics.

Apart from working in the CMC of Laitumkhrah Block A, Mawlong became an active member of the Catholic Students in Universities (CSU), an association of Catholic students that engaged in community service. An old friend and colleague, Andrew Ishohari, who was with Mawlong in college and in the CSU, recollected how he had helped to induct him into the association.

> Being with Bah Kek Mawlong was most elating. He had this uncanny knack of winning friends easily and he could speak confidently, yet in a very gentle and composed manner. Even in those past days, I could see leadership abilities in him as he could easily get along with people and get work done quickly. His ideas were also very different, so it didn't surprise me when he joined politics.

The year 1966 was extremely difficult for Mawlong as he contracted typhoid. Doctors at Nazareth Hospital had given up hope and they said it was a miracle that he survived. During the stay in the hospital, which lasted for months, the much-loved pupil felt the affection of many well-wishers.

One day, Marbaniang remembers that he bumped into the late Bishop Stephen Ferrando, and his secretary Fr Mario at the hospital. As he bent forward to kiss the Bishop's ecclesiastical ring on his finger, and as he rose to meet his gaze, he was delighted to see Fr Noel Joseph Kenny, the Vice Principal of St Anthony's College, and Fr Joseph Arokiaswamy, the Principal. When they entered the

general ward, Mawlong was lying down reading a book and on seeing them, he immediately cheered up. After formal greetings, everyone prayed together for the patients, including Mawlong.

> I remember the book he was reading was *The Shoes of the Fisherman* written by one ex-seminarian. Fr Kenny took the book from Bah Kek, flipped to its back cover and remarked, 'So Evansius, would you like to become a priest? A leader of souls?' Bah Kek smiled faintly and said, 'Father, perhaps there are many men who'd like to become priests, but I think there are few willing to join politics. Please pray for me, Father.'
> Bishop Ferrando prophetically said, 'You will live long, don't worry; you will one day become a leader of this land and its people.'

Because of his prolonged illness, Mawlong had to wait for another year to graduate in 1969. During his time in the college and later, he often visited his paternal relatives at Nongkseh, Upper Shillong. Most of Sajerson Thangkhiew's relatives stay in a row of houses at the place. Mawlong would often visit his aunt Emeliana Melis Thangkhiew and her sisters. He was also a frequent visitor to the family of his uncle Shan Roy Thangkhiew, who stayed close to Nongkseh in Lummawbah.

Shan Roy was the *Basan* or elected representative of Nongkseh village under Hima Mylliem or Mylliem Syiemship. He was more popularly called Shan Roy Basan because of the position he held till his demise. The Thangkhiew clan members elect

the Basan to represent them in the Syiem's[18] office. After Shan Roy Thangkhiew passed away, Emerson Thangkhiew, Sajerson Thangkhiew's youngest brother and Mawlong's paternal uncle, was elected as the Basan of Nongkseh.

One day, when Mawlong visited a school that was established by Shan Roy's family in 1956, he was told that the school needed a science teacher. He readily agreed to take up the position, continuing his close association with his paternal family. His time at the school also allowed him to work closely with JE Tariang, the son-in-law of Shan Roy, who was to later represent Meghalaya as a member of the Rajya Sabha (1985-91). Tariang was already active in politics as an elected member in the United Khasi-Jaiñtia Hills Autonomous District Council in 1952–57, and was also the publisher of the weekly vernacular newspaper *U Pyrman*. Mawlong taught in the school and later became the editor of the paper. He was fond of reading and writing from his school days. It was during his regime as the editor of *U Pyrman* that his interest strengthened in politics. His personal rapport and working relationship with JE Tariang, who was an active member of the Congress Party in Meghalaya, further increased his interest in pursuing a career in public service.

18 A Syiem is a ruler and administrator of a traditional Khasi state or kingdom

A year before he graduated, Mawlong joined St Dominic Savio High School, Mawkhar, Shillong as a teacher of mathematics and science in the English section as he waited for his BSc results. As his days in college were over, he moved out of Stephen Hall and took up rented accommodation at Mawkhar Mission Compound in Shillong. His rented house was a single-floor Assam-type cottage and his owner, whom they fondly called Bei Wong, rented out three partitioned rooms.

The house was very close to the school, and so he walked every day through the Mawkhar Main Road. One of his students, KM Warjri recalls that as a teacher, he could simplify hard concepts.

> Babu was a friendly and cheerful person. There was never a time when we saw him serious or overly strict and imposing authority upon his students. There were days when the regular teachers did not turn up to take class. So he'd walk into our classroom and say, 'What should I teach you? If I teach, I might unnecessarily confuse you because teachers have their own style of teaching. I will tell you a story instead'.

Warjri remarks that the students loved how Mawlong's stories broke the monotony of academics. His stories revolved around cowboys, horse riders and gunfights and were often in the style of Louis L'Amour, the American novelist and short story

writer famous for his Western genre of novels.

> We would visualise the scenes from cowboy movies; images of men in cowboy hats who rode horses with pistols in hand completely enthralled all of us. He'd often put a condition that the stories would be told only if we completed our work and were at our best behaviour. One character that I remember from his stories was Johnny Ringo.

Since the 1970s were the years of rock and roll, like most of the country, Shillong was also influenced by the West, particularly in music and fashion. Like others from that era, Mawlong sported the Beatle Cut like Ringo Starr and John Lennon. The Mop Top haircut covered his ears. Besides, he wore bell-bottoms and printed shirts. Whenever the students met Mawlong on the roads of Mawkhar or Jaïaw, he'd pat them and crack a joke. Since he was approachable and friendly, he was given a nickname, Bu Ringo. Even today, the students of St Dominic's School of that generation remember him by his nickname, says Warjri.

A year after he graduated, Mawlong's mother passed away. Her funeral took place at Mawmih, and a memorial stone that the family erected still exists at the clan-owned graveyard in the village.

Mawlong resigned from St Dominic Savio School in early 1971 to work in the Accountant General's Office (AG's Office) as an Upper Divisional Assistant. Although he enjoyed his work as a teacher, the inadequate pay was the primary

reason for his resignation. Apparently, his request for a raise wasn't acceded.

His tenure in the AG's Office lasted only about six months. By that time, he was already actively involved as a volunteer in the church's social outreach programmes, which accorded him the opportunity to work closely with Peter G Marbaniang, Martin N Majaw, and John D Pohrmen, who were his teachers and prominent political leaders of the Hill State Movement, and active members of the Catholic Church. Mawlong's plunge into politics can be attributed to his growing interest in social work as an active member of the church. Although he didn't occupy any prominent designated post as such, he played an instrumental role in organising the youth of the church to take part in various commemorative events. After passing out from college, he was actively involved in the Don Bosco Past Pupils' Association. As a young leader of the church's social organisations, he had the opportunity to help those who were financially weak, to extend support to such individuals and families. Like his mother, he was driven by a desire to alleviate people's distress.

Since he was among a handful of educated young men in Mawmih, the unchanged condition of the villagers affected Mawlong. He had the desire to change the destiny of the villagers, most of whom were poor peasants, through political empowerment and intervention. In the few

months that he had spent in the AG's Office, he felt a growing restlessness and discontentment.

By the time Mawlong decided to join politics, Emerson Thangkhiew, his paternal uncle was already an elected member of the United Khasi-Jaiñtia Hills District Council in 1958 and again in 1967 from Sohïong constituency. Thangkhiew's presence in politics and considerable vote bank in the Diengïei area as a Member of the District Council was an important factor that motivated Mawlong to contest the first election to the Meghalaya Legislative Assembly of the newly created state of Meghalaya in 1972.

FIRST STEPS IN POLITICS

AFTER INDIA'S independence from British rule in 1947 and its adoption of the Constitution on 26 January 1950, the country was organised into a 'Union of States'. The hill areas of the North-East were initially included in the state of Assam with Shillong as the capital.

Assam, like most of the new Indian states, was accorded a separate state Legislative Assembly. The people of the Khasi-Jaiñtia and Garo Hills elected representatives from their respective regions to the Assam Legislative Assembly. This was a practice from the time when Assam was a province during the British rule. The most eminent representatives from the Khasi-Jaiñtia Hills were Rev JJM Nichols Roy, Lar Sing Khyriem, Kong Mavis Dunn Lyngdoh, and Kong Bonnily Khongmen. Along with the Legislative Assembly, a provision in the Sixth Schedule of the Indian Constitution mandated the formation of Autonomous District Councils in the Hill areas of Assam, including the Khasi-Jaiñtia and Garo Hills, inhabited predominantly by the Scheduled Tribes.

The mastermind behind the creation of the Autonomous District Councils was Reverend JJM Nichols Roy, an eminent elected member of the Constituent Assembly, who was originally from Shella in the Khasi Hills. The members of the Constituent Assembly were indirectly elected to frame the Constitution of India as proposed by British India's Cabinet Mission Plan in 1946. In a series of discussions in the Assembly, Rev Roy proposed the introduction of a provision in the Indian Constitution which would guarantee the creation of District Councils where the hill people of the North-East and other parts of the country would be given certain measures of self-governance primarily to safeguard the unique tribal customs and practices. A complete amalgamation of the tribal areas in the territory of India without such safeguards would endanger the survival of their customary practices, Rev Roy felt. The introduction of the District Councils enabled the people of United Khasi Jaiñtia Hills, Garo Hills, Naga Hills, Lushai Hills, North Cachar Hills and the Mikir Hills to elect representatives to these councils, which enjoyed certain legislative, executive and judicial powers.

Rev Roy was also motivated by a desire to make the customary tribal institutions more democratic.

Although the customary political establishment, particularly in the Khasi-Jaiñtia Hills, is not autocratic because of the autonomy the clans, *durbar*,[19] village, and *raid*[20] enjoy the hereditary succession by a family or clan to Syiemship and other high offices in the Khasi states, did not allow a democratic involvement. The introduction of the District Councils, Rev Roy felt, would ensure the existence of constitutionally valid bodies that would safeguard the traditional institutions and customary practices. The Sixth Schedule was Rev Roy's landmark contribution not only to the Khasi-Jaiñtia region, but to the tribal-dominated areas of the North-East, as it provides an opportunity to the public, including women, to take part in legislative and executive processes with a mandate to preserve the unique customary practices. Rev Roy's demand for the creation of Autonomous District Councils in the hill areas of Khasi, Jaiñtia, Garo, Lushai (Mizo), North Cachar, among others did bear fruit, but the elected leaders of the autonomous councils and other prominent legislators in the Assam Legislative Assembly, felt that it was insufficient to safeguard the interests of the hill people, and mooted demand for the creation of a separate state.

The demand for a separate state began to escalate in the late 1950s largely due to the tribals'

19 Elected council of a village
20 Cluster of villages

resistance to the cultural and linguistic imposition of the Assamese majority. The Assamese-speaking majority of the state instituted a demand to secure recognition of Assamese as the official language of the entire state of Assam. As Assam comprised a large number of tribal-dominated areas like the Khasi, Jaiñtia, Garo, Lushai (Mizo), and Naga Hills, and a Bengali-speaking majority in the Barak Valley districts of Cachar, Hailakandi, and Karimganj, the proposal, which was spearheaded by the Assam Sahitya Sabha, was resented by the non-Assamese speaking communities. There was already discontent among the tribal leaders because only Assamese gained recognition as an Official Language in the Eighth Schedule of the Constitution of India, despite the existence of unique tribal dialects and languages. However, the Assam Sahitya Sabha continued to spread its supremacy in various administrative units of the state. The non-Assamese residents of Assam countered the demand with mass protests, particularly in Bengali-dominated Silchar, and also in Shillong, Hailakandi, and Karimganj. Pro-Assamese groups and even political entities like the Assam Provincial Congress Committee (APCC), which was the state unit of the Congress Party, demanded from the Chief Minister of Assam, Bimala Prasad Chaliha, to implement the Language Act to make Assamese the official language of Assam. The Chief Minister acceded to their demand and presented a Bill in

the Assam Legislature mandating Assamese as the only official language of Assam. The Bill was passed in the legislature on 24 October 1960 amidst protest from the Bengali-speaking elected members of the Assembly. Widespread public protest resulted with the calling of bandhs and processions. The mass movement was largely non-violent till an ill-fated incident that occurred on 19 May 1961. On the fateful day, the Cachar Zila Gana Sangram Parishad, a group spearheading the protests against the introduction of Assamese as the official language in the Barak Valley, organised a non-violent protest rally which later spiralled out of control. The security forces resorted to *lathi* (baton) charge to disperse the swelling mob, but when the tense situation could no longer be contained, they opened fire leading to the death of eleven protestors.[21]

After this unfortunate incident, the Assam Government had to withdraw the Bill, and later in 1967, introduced Bengali as an official language in three districts of the Barak Valley: Cachar, Hailakandi, and Karimganj.

The Language Movement had its effect on the hill areas too, but the dissension against the Assam Government had started even before that because the hill leaders felt that the District Councils

21 https://web.archive.org/web/20130529232759/http://wethepeople-barakvalley.com/bhasha-shahid-divas-language-martyrs%E2%80%99-day/843

weren't sufficient to safeguard their interests, and wanted more autonomy in shaping the political destiny of their people

Captain Willamson Ampang Sangma of the Garo Hills Autonomous District Council emerged as one of the most prominent political leaders to accelerate the demand for a separate state for the Khasi, Jaiñtia and Garo people. In the Khasi Hills, leaders such as William Reade, Hoover Hynñiewta, LG Shullai, BB Lyngdoh, Hopingstone Lyngdoh, GG Swell were the prominent political figures who spearheaded mass campaigns to petition the central Government to separate the hill areas from Assam.

The introduction of the Language Bill by the Chief Minister in the Assembly led to Capt Sangma convening a large congregation of hill leaders from various political parties in Shillong to oppose it. All hill leaders, including those from the Congress party, were united on their opposition to the Bill.[22] At the meeting, the hill leaders unanimously organised themselves into a single entity named the All Party Hill Leaders' Conference (APHLC) whose main objective was to demand for separation of the hill areas from Assam. Although initially their focus was to solely oppose the implementation of the Language Bill, by their third meeting, the APHLC

22 Kumar, Nikhlesh (May–August 2005), 'Identity Politics in the Hill Tribal Communities in the North-Eastern India' , Sociological Bulletin, Indian Sociological Society, 54 (2): 195–217, doi:10.1177/0038022920050203

demanded the formation of a separate state.

A series of meetings were held between the central ministers and the hill leaders to reach a consensus. At first, Pandit Jawaharlal Nehru opposed the demand and was ready to grant more autonomy to the hill areas, but they didn't agree. Negotiations continued with subsequent central governments after Nehru's death. The movement for a separate state gained considerable support from the general public who enthusiastically participated in peaceful demonstrations. Their efforts bore fruit with the passage of the Assam Reorganisation Act, enacted on 2 April 1970, leading to the creation of an Autonomous State of Meghalaya.

The new autonomous state had a separate legislature with thirty-seven members, which functioned in accordance with the provisions of the Sixth Schedule of the constitution. A minor setback occurred by way of a split in the APHLC with the expulsion of Hopingstone Lyngdoh, a fiery youth leader of the APHLC. Lyngdoh didn't agree with the APHLC's decision to accept the status of an autonomous region. Lyngdoh initially formed the Hill State Volunteers Adhoc Committee (HSVAC) in 1968 and later the Hill State People's Democratic Party (HSPDP) in 1969. Finally, after many negotiations and peaceful protests, the then Prime Minister Indira Gandhi conceded the long-standing peaceful demand with the inauguration of a full-fledged state of Meghalaya on 21 January

1972 with a Legislative Assembly comprising sixty legislators. The Autonomous District Councils were also retained and the United Khasi-Jaiñtia Hills Autonomous District Councils were bifurcated into the Khasi Hills Autonomous District Councils and Jaiñtia Hills Autonomous District Councils. In the same year, the new states of Manipur and Tripura were also created.

In the inaugural year of 1972, two elections were held in Meghalaya: an election to the Legislative Assembly in March, and another to the two District Councils (United Khasi and Jaiñtia Hills District Council, and Garo Hills District Council) in May. In the latter part of 1971, Mawlong prepared himself to contest the elections from the newly demarcated Assembly constituency named Umroi. Hopingstone Lyngdoh's new party had gained considerable support and was a serious contender to the APHLC. Mawlong had initially sought a party ticket from the HSPDP, but was denied. As he was a new entrant without much direct political participation, he opted to contest as an Independent.

Mawlong's intention to fight the General Election to the new state Legislative Assembly got support from Kenny Nongbsap, a Minister of Hima Mylliem,[23] and also a rich trader, who was Mawlong's brother-in-law's uncle. Nongbsap

23 Traditional kingdom of Mylliem

understood the financial implications of the political campaign particularly for travelling from one place to another. He provided Mawlong a jeep and a driver so he could travel to the most remote places in Umroi as most of the settlements in those days were far from one another and the area was extremely vast with deplorable road conditions.

In that first general election to the Legislative Assembly, the area of the Umroi constituency was very vast though the voters were comparatively fewer. The constituency comprised villages starting from Dira village in Mawphlang, all along Weilengkut, Nongpathaw, Lawmei, Mawmih, Kreit, Mawlyndep, Umbir, Umiam, Umroi, Bhoirymbong, Raid Madan Kyrdem, Lumsohphoh, Umrynjah and others, which were all part of the East Khasi Hills District. Because of the various delimitation exercises that the Election Commission undertook in later years, most of these villages are now in present-day Sohiong, Umsning, or Mawhati constituencies.

There were six candidates who contested from Umroi, but the most formidable opponent was Dlosing Lyngdoh (Bah Dlo) of the Indian National Congress (INC). Bah Dlo, a resident of Khapmara village near Bhoirymbong, was senior in age and experience. Although young Mawlong and his associates had campaigned hard for his victory, he couldn't emerge victorious and fell short by a mere fifty votes. When the votes were counted on

9 March, Bah Dlo polled 908, and Mawlong 858.

Hari Mawlong, Evansius Kek Mawlong's first cousin, believes that his cousin would have won had it not been for Medras Mylliem. Hari Mawlong says that both Evansius Kek Mawlong and Mylliem belonged to the Diengïei area and they were related through marriage. When news spread the two were likely to go head-to-head, the elder relatives arranged a meeting to urge Mylliem against contesting as it could result in both of them losing, and more importantly, it could create a rift within the family. As Mylliem was only an in-law, he was urged to sit out and support Mawlong, a son of the Diengïei area. Initially, Mylliem had readily agreed before the relatives, but to everyone's surprise, a few weeks before the election, he announced his candidature from the Hill State People's Democratic Party (HSPDP), the same party which had denied Mawlong a party ticket. Mylliem reasoned that it was the party that had pressurised him to contest. Hari Mawlong says that had only one of them contested, the votes wouldn't have split, and had Mylliem stuck to his word, Evansius Kek Mawlong could have won his first election.

Though dejected by the narrow loss, Mawlong and his supporters didn't lose heart. The margin of defeat enticed him to fight another election. The twenty-six-year-old greenhorn did not expect to get so many votes in the first place, so was happy with his performance because the contest was against

Bah Dlo who had an excellent support base. Kenny Nongbsap, who worked hard in that election was the most disappointed, as he campaigned in the Diengïei area with all his heart and soul. He encouraged Mawlong to fight the District Council elections scheduled in that same year. But Mawlong was reluctant as he had spent most of his money in that election and contesting another would mean using up the one thousand rupees that he was left with. Nongbsap, though, didn't agree and insisted that Mawlong should give it one more try as he was hopeful that he would be second-time lucky. He readily financed him the second time too.

However, before the commencement of the campaign for the District Council elections, another tussle within the family emerged.

The United Khasi and Jaiñtia Hills District Council, had had three prior elections in 1952, 1958 and 1967. Mawlong's paternal uncle, Emerson Thangkhiew was an elected Member of the District Council twice from the Sohiong constituency in the years 1958 and 1967. In the 1972 election, Emerson Thangkhiew was keen to contest from Umroi. Though it was a new constituency, most of his favoured villages were included in it. Mawlong felt he had a better chance of winning based on his previous experience. Uncertainty and confusion yet again prevailed over the candidature. Eventually they couldn't reach any consensus, so uncle and nephew went head-to-head against each other. Mawlong

and his supporters went from village to village urging people to vote for the young and educated man. He didn't pursue a ticket from any party, and went ahead to contest again as an Independent. His supporters worked day and night to ensure he attained the much desired goal.

After the declaration of results, without any hostility, Emerson Thangkhiew wound a traditional Khasi turban around the head of his nephew outside the counting hall at the State Central Library in Shillong and said, 'It's now your turn, son. The people have favoured you above everyone else.'

Thus it was that Evansius Kek Mawlong's long association with the people of Umroi began with his election as an Independent representative of the 15-Umroi constituency in the Khasi Hills Autonomous District Council on 10 May 1972.

THRUST ON EDUCATION

AS AN Independent member in the District Council, the young EK Mawlong, chose not to join the new CEM's Executive Committee (EC) and did not hold the post of Executive Member. The decision to sit in the Opposition enabled him to take part in the discussions of the House; giving suggestions and vociferous critiques. Being in the ruling EC would have deprived him of such an opportunity. He presented his views in a lucid and sensible manner. For instance, he lamented the incapability of the EC to manage the financial resources of the Council, urging it to 'try to get all its share (of funds) from the State Government,' as most of the council's financial resources are generated through royalty collected from mining and trade of minerals and other natural resources. The royalty is divided between the State Government and the Council, but the latter often suffers as the State Government often delays the release of the Council's share. The other major source of funds is from grants given by the Central Government from time to time. To improve the financial condition of the Council, he suggested that revenue could be earned from fishery. This innovative proposal may have been offered to the EC of the Council considering the insignificant number of fish farmers in the district. It was considered by Mawlong as a new avenue that could generate more revenue for the Council as fish farming was not widespread. He proposed that a separate department be created for the same and river guards be appointed to protect the fish. The Umïam Reservoir or Barapani could become a source of revenue and employment generation by building floating boats and floating restaurants, he suggested.

In most of his speeches he brought to the notice of the EC the deplorable plight of primary education, which was then under the control of the District Council. Being a former teacher himself, he often expressed dismay at the overall management of the education sector, particularly the pathetic treatment accorded to teachers. Apparently, the teachers were paid only once a year, according to a statement he made in 1972. He urged the Executive Council to explore possibilities of paying the teachers as frequently as possible. He was also perturbed to see teachers being made to stand in a long serpentine queue to collect their salary, and suggested measures to discontinue such a demeaning practice.

During the 1974 Budget Session, he brazenly criticised the Executive Committee for lack of vision, calling them 'a group of members who had no clear-cut policy' by citing instances from single-teacher schools where infrastructure was also inadequate. As per his narrative:

> One teacher has to teach 70-80 pupils. I was a teacher once, and I know how troublesome it is to have to do this. Yesterday, one teacher came to me and complained that he has 70 pupils and that he has to divide them into two groups and has to teach the same thing twice. The EC must think of ways to help such schools. In some schools, students have to sit on the floor because of the shortage of teachers.

Time and again he urged the EC of the day to take over more schools under its jurisdiction and have a clear-cut policy on how to improve the condition of schools, particularly in rural areas. He also stressed on the need to maintain parity in the schools as far as the student-teacher ratio was concerned, urging the EC's officers to 'inspect all schools so that parity is maintained'.

On 19 March 1975, he again highlighted the need to improve the plight of education, citing a growing demand for more schools and teachers. He acknowledged that shortage of funds was the fundamental reason for the Council's inability to completely meet the expectation of the people. They

could appoint not more than four or five teachers in a year, who were paid inadequately and untimely.

Apart from education, Mawlong argued about the need to arrest corruption and pilferage of revenue. He was also aware of the rules and procedures pertaining to the conduct of sessions and often raised concerns whenever the House ran contrary to the prescribed regulations.

Meanwhile in 1974-75, Mawlong took a significant decision by associating himself with the Congress party in the state. His closeness to Congressman JE Tariang, and association with Congress stalwarts Captain Williamson A Sangma and Purno A Sangma perhaps influenced his decision. Purno A Sangma was a college mate and close friend. In later years, both maintained cordial relations despite their different party affiliations. In September 1975, the Congress party unanimously elected Mawlong to lead the Meghalaya Pradesh Youth Congress succeeding former Legislator of Mahendraganj constituency, Captain Manik Das. He later became a member of the National Council of the Indian Youth Congress and took part in the sessions of the All Indian Congress Committee (AICC) in Shimla, Himachal Pradesh in 1975, and in Dispur, Assam in 1976. However, his stay in the party was short-lived and he resigned sometime in 1976-77. Mawlong often referred to his brief stint in the party and the inexplicable feeling of despondence and lack of belongingness in the Congress. Also, in the decade

following the attainment of statehood, the regional parties were very influential and popular in the Khasi and Jaiñtia Hills. The Congress was largely perceived to be an outsider's party, with little or no inclination to protect the interests of the tribal people. His core supporters in the constituency and friends who helped him in his electoral campaigns too, did not favour his continuance in the national party.

The protectionist movements and agitations to defend the indigenous people from the migrant non-indigenous populace has also been a subject of discourse in the state since the 1970s till date, particularly in the Khasi-Jaiñtia Hills. Mawlong often spoke in favour of such ideology as evident from his speeches in the Council. In 1977, he appealed to the EC to use the provisions of the Sixth Schedule of the Constitution of India to protect and preserve the Khasi indigenous culture. He reminded the members of the Council that the minuscule Khasi community would one day become extinct if measures were not taken to safeguard its people, particularly from the growing influx of illegal migrants from neighbouring Bangladesh. The 1971 war had just concluded and the nation witnessed large-scale migration of Bangladeshis to India. There was a growing fear that the Khasi race would slowly be wiped out if remedial steps were not taken. He urged the EC to take matters which were beyond its purview to the State Government, particularly to mitigate the

rise in influx, prevention of sale of land to non-tribals, and to frame laws that would discourage inter-marriage between tribals and non-tribals.

Concerning state-wide issues, the most pressing of all was the border dispute between Assam and Meghalaya that Mawlong tried to address to the best of his ability. After the bifurcation of Assam and creation of Meghalaya, the state boundaries were not clearly demarcated. Amidst the elation and enthusiasm of the leaders and people after achieving their desired goal of a separate State, the leaders of the All-Party Hill Leaders' Conference (APHLC) failed to set a clear-cut demarcated boundary between the two states.[24] Till date there are twelve areas of difference between the two states which remain unresolved. Frequent clashes still take place owing to encroachment from either side. Block II, which was under Umroi constituency, is among the twelve disputed areas between the two states and many villages, including Jatalong and Khlieh Umwang fall within it.

In the early 1970s, Phillip Duia, a resident of Mawkyrdep village heard that the Khasis had cut a cow near the Umwang Market, a popular destination for all communities of the area, including Nepali people from the Assam side of the border. Many alleged that the intention was primarily to antagonise the Nepali community,

24 https://nenow.in/north-east-news/meghalaya/can-meghalaya-get-back-356-villages-in-block-i-and-ii-from-assam.html

says Duia. Since the attainment of statehood, communal clashes leading to intervention and arrests of the Khasi villagers by the Assam police were common in Umwang, Sabuda and Jatalong border villages. Such altercations, and sometimes bloodshed, were not new and continue till this day. Since the issue of territorial dispute was heated, the violence was frequent and unpredictable.

During those days, there was no road connecting Umroi-Bhoirymbong area to the Block II villages near Assam. There was only one route, which was through a cluster of villages around Kyrdem village and vehicles were also few. Both sides had prepared themselves with knives and arrows to defend their communities.

> I don't know how Bah Heh Kek got the news of the prevailing dissension. He rushed to my house from Shillong, and together we went to meet Babu M Dliton Shadap, who was his teacher at Kreit village when he was very young. It was late to go to Umwang that day, so Bah Heh Kek stayed back at my place. He told me, 'The police already know about the problem, and they must have taken control of the situation for now. But we should go there and try to pacify things so that trouble doesn't erupt again when the police leave.

The next morning, the three walked from Mawkyrdep facing a heavy downpour and leeches to reach Ïew Umwang. At a tea stall, they got to

know that Government authorities from Meghalaya and Assam had already arrived. When Mawlong, as a Member of the District Council (MDC) met the Meghalaya official, P Mulieh, he was told to gather the people for a durbar and summon the leaders of both the communities to resolve matters in the open. Mawlong feared that unless this was done in an open manner, both communities will spare no time to kill each other. Fortunately, the leaders signed a peace agreement.

> At the end, Bah Heh Kek gave a speech where he said, 'As of now, the villages Umtlih, Umwang, Umlaper, Jatalong, and Sabuda fall under the disputed area. The governments of Assam and Meghalaya are yet to solve this problem. Until they find a solution, all of you should live in harmony. Do not instigate misunderstanding; do not promote bloodshed.'

Mawlong had a soft corner for the poor and downtrodden. The days when dispute in the Block II areas escalated, the men of the villages would flee for their lives, fearing retaliation from the villagers or arrest by the Assam police.

In such uncertain times, they would dash to Shillong to seek refuge in Mawlong's rented house and returned only after normalcy was restored. He also made sure to visit the people in need. Whether someone fell sick, or a house caught fire, he ensured to visit the people.

Mawlong was moved by the abject poverty in which people lived, says Duia. Apart from arranging for mortuary vans and ambulances, Mawlong would always find something comforting to say to the poverty-stricken people. Unlike the urban constituencies where most people have access to better healthcare facilities, a rural constituency has its own challenges. People need guidance and empathy.

> In such times, he was never alone and always ensured a friend or supporter accompanied him. Babu Dliton Shadap of Mawkyrdep; Sentina Lyngdoh of Umiam; Allan Wahlang, D Talukdar, and Wilkinson Jala of Umroi were his constant companions. He never hesitated to stay back at any of his friends' houses and had this gift of making people feel at ease. Perhaps because of his village upbringing, he was like one of us.

As evident from his speeches in the District Council, Mawlong believed strongly in education and even helped his niece study in a private school in Shillong. He looked after the needs of both Erimai Mawlong, who was the daughter of Isidora, and those of Eloris Mawlong, daughter of Jnger Mawlong, his eldest sister. They stayed with him in the rented house in Mission Compound.

Mawlong had already admitted Eloris Mawlong, whose pet name was Mem, when he asked his sister to allow him to admit Erimai in school.

Isidora says that her brother's plan to relocate her young daughter to Shillong worried her as the child was only seven years old. She was worried that her daughter would find it difficult to adjust in the new town, and to study in a school with students from better backgrounds. But the thought of a better future, after seeing her own brother succeed in life thanks to a good education, made her give in.

The seven-year-old Erimai Mawlong left Mawmih with her uncle as the village school had provision only till Class 3, thus limiting her prospect for further education. The little girl, like her mother, was petrified.

> 'What if the *dkhar*[25] in Shillong takes me away somewhere when you're not there?' she asked her uncle.
>
> 'No, no. Nothing like that will happen. I will take you to the big shops there where you'll find lots of good clothes and toys.'

Excited at the thought, the mother-daughter duo went to Shillong during the winter vacation to get familiar with the surroundings before joining St Joseph's School at Jaïaw.

In the absence of Mawlong, the landlady or sometimes Prof Khongwir and other friends who also lived close by, looked after them. Mawlong used to dote on the girls, giving them pocket money to buy goodies.

25 A term used for non-tribals from mainland India who come to Shillong and other parts of Khasi-Jaiñtia hills to earn a living

They would run to the nearby eateries wrapped in their *jaiñ tapmoh*[26] during the day.

> We were too timid to wander around the strange town. Being typical village girls, we would run from Mission Compound to Mawkhar. The friendly neighbours often taunted both of us as 'two identical ducks of Ward's Lake'[27] because we always wore similar shawls and clothes. Like normal children, we'd be elated whenever Mawlong bought new clothes for us once in a while. But people would laugh at us playfully, as most of them were oversized.

One day, Erimai felt homesick and longed for the carefree village life. When her mother visited her, she cried uncontrollably. The girl was consoled by her mother and together they left for the village in the absence of Mawlong. Two days later, she heard her uncle screaming her name. As the scared girl hid under the bed, she could see him holding a stick. A few hours later, he tried to assuage her fears and explain how studying in Shillong was for her benefit.

> 'Look at me,' he would always say encouragingly, 'do you want to become like me or not?' He always used that rhetorical question on me and later my siblings whom he brought from Mawmih to Shillong to study in various schools. That was the first and only escape plan I

26 Traditional Khasi shawl

27 An artificial lake in Shillong and popular tourist spot

executed unsuccessfully. I never returned to the village, except during holidays, till I completed my graduation. And in all those years, he would only hold a stick intimidatingly, but never really used it.

HALCYON DAYS

IT WAS the early 1970s when Mawlong met Chosterfield Khongwir, a man with myriad talents. Originally from Umsning village, Khongwir is a retired Professor of Khasi in St Edmund's College, Shillong and a renowned folk musician and folklorist. In the days before Mawlong joined politics, Prof Khongwir, being a keen anthropologist, had already documented the hazardous terrain of the Bhoi Lasa[28] and Raid Nongtung[29] area which fell under Umroi constituency.

Khongwir explored the hills of Ri Bhoi[30] like an intrepid researcher. He was fascinated by the farmers who would labour all day for a bountiful harvest in the lush green paddy fields. Their reverberating whistles and songs were music to his

28 Cluster of villages in Umroi constituency

29 Cluster of villages in Umroi constituency bordering Assam

30 Region inhabited predominantly by the Bhoi sub-group

ears. Although roads were almost non-existent, he walked for hours from one village to another.

> In the late 1960s, my research interest frequently took me to those distant villages. That resulted in cultivation of a familiar bonding with the people, more so because I learnt their dialect.

Mawlong's friendship with Prof Khongwir was forged during his MDC days at Mawkhar where the musician used to stay and later at Luisa Brosilla Lamin's place at Mawlai. Lamin was an Executive Member in the District Council, and Mawlong, as an MDC, frequented her place for some work or the other.

> Though I didn't know Bah Heh Kek well at that point, whenever we met, he'd wave his hand and call out to me, speaking in a manner as though we were already thick as thieves! Slowly, our friendship fostered and grew over endless cups of tea and many plates of fried noodles at Mawkhar.

Their love for music brought them closer. Khongwir remembers Mawlong would spontaneously croon to a Jim Reeves number. Mawlong used to play the clarinet well since his days in the Don Bosco Band in school. They would often sing in Mawlong's rented house at Mission Compound. Whenever he went to Umroi, it would take him long to return because of the poor condition of the roads. On such occasions, Khongwir would look after his nieces, Bih and Mem.

In February 1975, when Mawlong was a member of the Meghalaya Pradesh Youth Congress, he asked Khongwir to put up a musical performance in a cultural programme at the Congress Convention at Khanapara, Guwahati.

> If I remember correctly, the Congress organised it to felicitate Capt Williamson A Sangma when he formally joined the party after he had quit the APHLC. I was reluctant at first because I never wanted to interact with any political entity. It was out of my fondness for Bah Heh Kek that I agreed.

Khongwir gathered folk musicians and singers from all over the Bhoi area. The field was packed and reverberated with an original composition by Khongwir inspired by the harvesting of rice during winters:

'Er 'Er beh sha jan
Ah! to beh sha jan;
Pynher i'u stait nangne,
Pynher noh bran bran
(Breeze blow near /Blow near /Carry the chaff away from here/Carry it sooner).

After the programme, Mawlong was so elated that he hugged Khongwir the way only a gratified friend does.

Their friendship grew after the programme.

One evening, Mawlong told Khongwir to wait for his return from Umroi for he had something important to discuss.

> I had an inkling why he wanted to meet me. I was already very popular in the Bhoi areas and people even suggested contesting elections from there, but I wasn't keen at all. I was happy with making music; I still enjoy it, although I am old.

Khongwir had been approached by many others to help in election campaigns but he was reluctant.

> 'You know, Professor,' he said. That's how Mawlong always addressed Khongwir. 'I don't have any inclination to do routine monotonous office work. I feel my vocation is serving people this way.'
>
> 'But Bah Heh, it is a tough task. How many people can you look after?'
>
> 'That's a practical point. But I'd like to bring significant change. If you visit the villages in Diengïei area, like my village Mawmih, you will realise how poverty-stricken people are! The only means of income for most is brewing alcohol or working in the breweries as contracted labour. So I feel there is so much that I can do to change their lot.'

Mawlong added that he needed Khongwir's help to serve the people. He was to contest the MLA election in February 1978 and wanted to connect with the people. Since Khongwir was admired and respected by the people in the Umroi area and beyond, Mawlong hoped his campaign would be more impactful.

Though touched by his humility, Khongwir was still reluctant.

> 'But Bah Heh, I am an apolitical person. I don't understand politics at all. My interest is culture and music.'
>
> 'Look, we are two of us. I will do what I think I can do well. You do what you're great at. Charm the people with your songs; I will try to convince them with my speeches.'
>
> Khonwgir thought for a second before he confessed that there was another problem.
>
> 'What is it?'
>
> 'I don't think being with the Congress will help your cause.' Khongwir added that he was opposed to the political party.

Mawlong followed his advice and resigned from the Congress a year before the 1978 Legislative Assembly elections and contested solo as an Independent candidate. His dissatisfaction with the Congress ideology and discomfort within it further propelled his decision to leave the national party.

Having gained each other's trust, Mawlong and Khongwir started strategising on reaching out to the people to gain their support. They first visited

the office of the *Syiem*[31] of Mylliem[32] at Mawkhar to seek information about the number of *Raid*[33] in Umroi. Soon after, they began the campaign on Khongwir's motorbike. Khongwir says that even though Mawlong had gained considerable support from the people of the constituency as he was already an MDC, and won the confidence of local leaders and elders from the Umroi, Bhoirymbong and Kyrdem areas, he still needed to reach out into the interior villages, including Mawtneng, Mawbri, Liarkhla, Liarbang, Tyrso, Khlieh Umstem and also villages bordering the state of Assam like Sabuda, Jatalong, Ummat and Umlaper. Their goal was to win the support of the most vulnerable: the unemployed, the peasants, the daily wage earners. This meant that they had to often walk from one village to the next, often halting a night or two in people's homes. Khongwir remembers:

> I never forget those warm, friendly people who accepted us despite their pitiable conditions. Those days there were hardly any roads that led to the interior villages. The moment you crossed Khapmara village, there was absolutely no road worth remembering.

31 Customary head of the Khasi tribal administrative area of the Khasi-Jaiñtia Hills known as the Khasi State prior to the integration with the Indian Union. The institution of the Syiem is still active but is under the administrative control of the District Council.

32 An administrative and territorial jurisdiction of the Syiem in East Khasi Hills

33 Clusters of villages

A major obstacle he had to face was the villagers' perception of him as an outsider because he was not from there or any of the nearby villages. This sentiment was very strong in the Bhoi Lasa, Raid Kyrdem, Raid Iapngar and Raid Nongtung. He was from Mawmih that is in the Diengïei region, and in the elections after 1972, all those villages in Diengïei were no longer a part of Umroi constituency. Along with his supporters, Mawlong made a conscious attempt to dispel such propaganda.

The Raid Ïapngar and Bhoi Lasa areas were difficult to reach as there were hardly any proper roads. They were at a distance of almost 25 km from the more accessible areas of Mawkyrdep and Kyrdem villages. Vehicles that would visit Shillong once or twice a week could reach till Kyrdem village, and there was only one old Bedford Bus and four Willys Jeeps. On days when it was too late to return to Shillong, they would stay back at somebody's thatched house because there were hardly enough vehicles or tarred roads.

> We'd sleep on the rough bamboo parquets or recline on some hay strewn on mud floors. But I will never get the blissful, carefree days like those again. Not a worry in the world; we enjoyed ourselves. Being the entertainer wherever I go, I'd spontaneously pull out my guitar or *duitara*[34] and sing self-composed songs.

34 A four-stringed Khasi folk musical instrument

Khongwir would sing Mawlong's favourite composition, '*Da wan phi mo Bei Kha...*' Even after a tiring day, he would sing along, clapping his hands joyously.

The two friends would set out on a motorcycle till Mawkyrdep or Umtung village after which there were no tarred roads. Thereafter, they'd walk on foot to other villages. They always carried extra petrol in bottles, as there was no guessing when the tank would run dry. Whenever such a thing happened, which it did frequently, Mawlong being the pillion rider, would hold up a bottle which supplied fuel directly through a pipe to the bike's carburettor. In those days, the only existing petrol pump in the vicinity of Umroi was one in Umïam village, which was far from the other hamlets.

One day, Mawlong bumped into his former student KM Warjri at Jaïaw Langsning in Shillong.

Mawlong met him when he was returning from Robert Hospital at Jaïaw after visiting someone who was ill. When he saw that Warjri had many vehicles, he asked him if he could lend him one jeep for his tours to Umroi. Warjri told him that since the vehicles belonged to his parents, he would need to take his mother's permission.

Although Mawlong wanted to pay the hiring charges, Warjri's mother provided a vehicle and a driver too, without any charges. Mawlong was glad to use the jeep for his trips to the constituency two to three times a week. One day, when they were

returning to Shillong past midnight, the tired driver inadvertently fell asleep at the steering wheel. The jeep fell into a ditch near the Umïam police post. Fortunately, nobody was hurt.

After this accident, Mawlong asked Warjri to accompany him on tours as his driver.

> After that accident, Babu convinced my mother to let me drive on his trips to his constituency. I'm glad that he made that decision because for at least fifteen years thereafter, I never left his side. And now, after so many years, I often go back to reopen the pages of those memorable chapters as I would a favourite classic song. No matter how many times I revisit those memorable years, I never get bored, and it only grows fonder with age.

Prof Khongwir used to travel with the duo, especially for big meetings. Warjri's job was to set up the sound system and Khongwir would sing to draw villagers to the venue.

> On hearing his voice on the loudspeaker, people would drop whatever work they were doing, and run to see and hear him. He was the crowd-puller. Babu[35] Kek, being an excellent orator, would then give speeches. But the people were often more interested in the songs! That was the drill in most public meetings.

35 Teacher

Those days, it was easy to identify who was a supporter. People used to be simple and never had to suppress their views. Warjri remembers how one of the most loyal supporters Duh Sen [Sentina Lyngdoh] became hostile towards a rival candidate.

A rival candidate had verbally abused Mawlong in a public meeting and when Duh Sen and her accomplices heard the same, they followed the candidate to his meeting.

> While he was giving a speech, Duh Sen calmly walked up to the dais and then all of a sudden the loudspeakers reverberated when her right palm landed on his cheek with a loud smack. Later, the women had to cool their heels at Umïam police post for a few hours.

Warjri adds that election campaigns used to get quite heated. In the 1978 election, when the trio were on their way to Kyrdem village, a rival camp group ambushed the jeep in which they were travelling. Mawlong's vehicle was pelted with rods and stones at Bhoirymbong market. Warjri managed to get away past the indignant crowd. Soon after the Bhoirymbong incident, Mawlong started to occupy the middle of the front seat as another occupant took the window seat for his safety. Despite the unexpected animosity, the 1978 campaign went well, says Warjri.

On counting day, a pessimistic Warjri was restless and chose not to go to the counting venue

at the State Central Library. Since counting was done on paper-ballots, the process would begin in the morning at about seven and continue late into the night.

Around one o'clock, Warjri heard people rejoicing in loud voices near his gate. He thought that the supporters of sitting MLA Dlosing Lyngdoh had gathered to not just celebrate Mawlong's loss and but also drag him out of the house. Everyone knew Warjri as he was always seen with Mawlong. When he drew the lace curtain slightly to peep out of the window of his living room, he could not recognise the faces walking down the driveway. He heard them knock thrice on the door and gathering courage he yanked the door's curtains wide apart. Instead, he saw three familiar faces. It was Duh Sen along with two friends.

> 'Bah Duh!' she screamed, lips parted in glee.
>
> 'What are you doing here?' Warjri asked, opening the door.
>
> 'Why are you in your pyjamas? Go wear your trousers! Bah Kek has won!'
>
> 'Why are you pulling my leg at this hour, Duh?'
>
> 'Do you think I'm joking? There he is,' she pointed towards the gate, 'look at the turban on his head!'

When Warjri looked up, he could see Mawlong hurrying down the steep driveway with a traditional

Jaiñ Spong Khor[36] spun around his head, his neck bejewelled with the Khasi *paila*[37]. The men he saw were Mawlong's supporters.

> He called out to me, but I went back inside the house to put on a decent pair of trousers. By then the dancing troupe, waving blue flags with the rising sun as the emblem, had descended inside our compound. Babu and I embraced and laughed in glee. That moment is forever etched in my memory.

Warjri and Mawlong then drove down to Umroi along with the others who had come in trucks and jeeps. Everyone was dancing in the vehicles, singing songs till dawn, welcoming a new day.

The event Warjri so vividly recollected was significant as it propelled Mawlong's long career in politics. It was through friends like Prof Chosterfield and KM Warjri, and other prominent supporters from Umroi like Duh Sen, Allan Wahlang, Wilkinson Jala and others that his first major election campaign in 1978 was a successful one. Thereafter, for at least another twenty-five years, he retained his seat, leaving an endless stream of memories that are often reignited by those who worked closely with him, particularly in his effort to usher positive change in the lives of the people of Umroi.

36 Golden silk turban

37 Necklace made of red coral and foil-covered beads in parallel strings

DE FACTO LEADER OF OPPOSITION

MEGHALAYA HAS an unenviable record of having State Governments with uncertain lifespans. The formation and survival of governments is usually the culmination of hectic politicking. In the first general election in 1972 after attaining statehood, three major political parties had contested and won: the APHLC, the Indian National Congress (INC) and the HSPDP, along with a few independent members. Prior to the election, the APHLC and the Congress had already had an understanding that in the event of a favourable result, the two parties would come together to form the first Government in the state. And the results indeed went in their favour. The APHLC, which was the strongest and most popular political party, won 32 seats and the INC 9 in the 60-member house.

Capt Williamson A Sangma of the APHLC was sworn in as the first Chief Minister of the State. However, in 1976, the Chief Minister deserted the APHLC, the party that he along with other hill state leaders had formed to attain a separate State, and joined the Congress along with a group of MLAs. Capt Sangma continued as Chief Minister until the end of the term in early 1978. Thereafter, under his able leadership, the Congress party scaled impressive heights in the subsequent elections, particularly in the Garo Hills. Though the Khasi-Jaiñtia Hills were strongholds of the APHLC and other regional political entities, the Congress slowly began to make inroads thanks to the growing mistrust among the masses, due to frequent defections and splits in the APHLC.

The APHLC had been the foremost regional political party of the state, and had a host of influential intellectuals. But the seeds of dissent and discontentment, largely because of the clash of opinions and quest for supremacy among the top leadership, led to its ultimate downfall. For instance, after the emergence of the HSPDP in 1969, another faction led by Prof GG Swell split from the APHLC in 1977 to form the Public Demands Implementation Convention (PDIC). The discord between the regional party leaders continued well into the 1980s and 1990s as more split factions and political parties emerged.

After the Assembly elections in 1978, Mawlong along with other elected members took the oath of affirmation administered by the Protem Speaker, Capt Sangma on 14 March. Unlike the result in

1972, the split in 1978 complicated the situation. From a mere nine seats in 1972, the Congress returned as the single-largest party with twenty-five seats. However, it did not stake claim to form the Government. On counting day, there was a popular demand from the people gathered outside the counting venue in Shillong to install a non-Congress Government. The supporters of the three parties marched together on the streets, waving the flags of the three regional parties-the APHLC, the PDIC and the HSPDP-tied together as a symbol of unity. Owing to public demand, the leaders of the parties eventually came together to discuss the possibility of forming a Government. The APHLC with sixteen legislators, PDIC's two, HSPDP's fourteen, and Mawlong (Independent) huddled together in the Assembly to find a way forward.

However, there was a tussle as they could not unanimously decide as to who should become the new Chief Minister. The tussle was between BB Lyngdoh and DD Pugh of the APHLC. Both Lyngdoh and Pugh were highly knowledgeable, respected and senior leaders of the APHLC who had taken active part in the statehood movement. After a seemingly endless discussion, the party members found a novel yet effective way to resolve the issue, i.e., lottery. After the draw, eventually, Darwin D Pugh was elected as leader of the three parties to become the second Chief Minister of the State. As per other accounts, Pugh had more

support from the APHLC legislators of Garo Hills. Though a Khasi, he was fluent in the Garo language, providing the comfort of a multi-lingual leader. To the supporters' joy, a new Government named *Ka Sorkar Lai Lama* or the Three-Flag Government was sworn in on 10 March 1978.

However, the following year, the three-party alliance collapsed when the Government broke ties with the HSPDP on 21 February 1979. Pugh of the APHLC continued as Chief Minister with the support of the PDIC and Independents. The second Pugh Ministry appointed Mawlong as a Minister of State but his stint was brief as the Government barely lasted five months, succumbing on 6 May 1979. BB Lyngdoh split from the APHLC with a section of MLAs and joined hands with his earlier bête noire, Captain Sangma of the Congress to form a new Government under the banner United Meghalaya Parliamentary Democratic Forum. The two agreed to share the Chief Minister's post for an equal tenure of two years.

Thus, Lyngdoh became the third Chief Minister of the state from 7 May 1979 to 7 May 1981 and Capt Sangma, for the second time in his chequered career, took over from 1981 till 1983. Lyngdoh's craft in stitching together such atypical alliances earned him the famous moniker, 'Father of Coalition Politics' and another rather pejorative eponym 'Mr Split'.

After the fall of Pugh's ministry, Mawlong did

not join BB Lyngdoh or Capt Sangma but asserted his role as an outspoken Opposition member. From then on, in his near 30-year career as a Legislator, he spent more than half his tenure on the Opposition benches. In the initial years, he raised several vital issues that afflicted the people of his constituency and in other parts of Ri Bhoi District,[38] alongside the witty Prof Martin N Majaw. He actively participated in Assembly sessions by bringing resolutions, cut motions, call attention motions, and the like, and highlighted what he perceived as the subsequent governments' indifference to people's problems. Although some of his ideas were not taken seriously, he was able to act upon them during 2000-01, when he was the Chief Minister, including seriously pursuing the border dispute with Assam, reclaiming land from defence forces, among others.

Bringing Administration Closer to the People

In the Budget Session of 1980, Mawlong brought a resolution recommending a separate administrative unit to be created comprising areas lying in the South-Eastern part of the Ri Bhoi Sub-Division as there was a proposal to shift the headquarter

38 A district which was carved out of East Khasi Hills in June 1992. Currently, there are five assembly constituencies under it – Nongpoh, Umroi, Mawhati, Jirang, and Umsning. Before the inauguration of the district in 1992, it was only Sub-Division with its headquarters at Umsning, which was later shifted to Nongpoh.

of the Sub-Division from Umsning to Nongpoh. Considering the vast distance of almost 60 km between the Western Ri Bhoi area of Nongpoh, and the Eastern side of Umroi and Mawhati, Mawlong vehemently opposed the move, citing its effects on the people because Nongpoh was much farther than Umsning. Alternatively, he demanded a complete bifurcation of the Western Ri Bhoi areas of Nongpoh and Umsning from the Eastern side of Mawhati and Umroi to hasten the administrative processes.

The creation of two additional districts in June 1992, namely, South Garo Hills and Ri Bhoi, was felt to be inadequate as Mawlong further advocated for the creation of a Civil Sub-Division in the areas falling in the Eastern side of Ri Bhoi District. The demand for the creation of a separate Civil Sub-Division was again rekindled in 1995 and 1997. However, this repeated demand remains unfulfilled till today. As of July 2018, a fresh demand for the creation of separate sub-divisions was made by the representatives of Jirang, Mawhati and Umroi from the incumbent Government.

Since his first election as an Independent member of the house during the 1978-83 term, Mawlong exhibited a typical regionalist approach, exhibiting what American political scientist, Myron Weiner believed was a 'nativist and son-of-the-soil' ethos, admonishing against the perceived challenges posed by non-indigenous mainstream forces that usurped the rights and land of the natives. Weiner,

a renowned academician and scholar, conducted an extensive study on ethnicity and migration in India in the late 1970s.

Reclaiming Land from Defence Authorities

Among several related issues opposed by Mawlong was the construction of a Military Complex at Rangmen in Umroi. There was a public outcry against the acquisition of land for the complex which forced the Ministry of Defence to reconsider the stoppage of the construction of the complex at Rangmen. However, the construction work did not halt. The main lifeline between Guwahati and Shillong, GS Road, had been cut to carry drinking water to this camp. The matter was first brought to the attention of the Assembly by Prof Majaw in 1982. Though on many occasions resolutions were passed in the Assembly urging the Central Government to halt the construction or to shift the location, there was no serious pursuit on the matter. Mawlong reminded the MLAs about the important resolutions that had been unanimously adopted in the House requesting the Government of India to shift the present Rangmen Cantonment Complex to another location. He lamented that there was no action and the Defence authorities had already acquired more than 3,000 acres of land at Rangmen and also wanted to acquire an additional 800 acres at Umden-Umroi near the Airport, Umrynjah, Umphrew, Umsahkhar and Lumshyiap.

> Mr Speaker, Sir, I voice my protest against any intention of further acquisition of land by the Defence authorities in that area. We must try to get back this acquired land of 3,000 acres and we must put a big full stop to any further acquisition of any land by the Defence authorities in that area.

In the same speech, Mawlong stressed on the need to decongest Shillong and urged the Government to negotiate with the Armed Forces to part with land in the capital city.

> The city of Shillong is so congested and we have to expand it. But where do we expand when the entire area has been covered by the Defence authorities, their buildings and offices? Look at Ïewduh and Ïew Mawlong; there is no place for parking of vehicles. So, why don't we also take up this question with the Central authorities, to ask for some more land, the unutilised land, and then expand at least the Motor station or parking area and so on and so forth?

He added that it was difficult to convince the Central authorities, as had been pointed out by some members, 'it is like meeting a rock.'

In the Autumn Session in 1996, he again spoke out against unabated land acquisition and alleged corruption prevailing in the cantonment areas. He feared that since more than fifty percent of the land in Shillong was occupied by the military and para-military forces, Shillong 'might be the main target in case there is war.'

Mawlong said that land for the Rangmen Cantonment 'was given in the early seventies' and 'compensation was made sometime in 1971 to 1973.' Although he along with the villagers, tried to take up the matter, it was too late.

> Land was already acquired to the military and our main point of objection was why so much land was given to the military, to the army in Shillong. Now, Ri-Bhoi, East Khasi Hills and other areas was being concentrated by the army. For Ri-Bhoi cantonment, they acquired 3,000 acres of prime land.

Mawlong lamented that although he raised objections to the Rangmen Complex since the year 1980, there was another move in 1981 to acquire an additional area of 800 acres, apparently to construct a firing range. He vehemently opposed the move along with the villagers who were going to be displaced. Much of the intended land that was to be acquired was fertile arable land fed by the perennial Umïam river. When he raised the issue in the Assembly, he compared the situation to that of Luckier Road in Shillong, where the Cantonment Board kept giving permissions to businessmen to construct buildings to expand their business without considering the growing congestion in the city.

> The officer concerned in the Cantonment Board has given permission to construct all these illegal buildings. On the other hand, the Government does not sincerely take

any effort... It appears that the business people are too strong a force to fight against here in Shillong. We have been crying for parking vehicles coming from... Umroi, Mawhati, Jirang and Nongpoh, there is no place to park vehicles...'

Subsequent governments disregarded the proposition to negotiate with the authorities of the Armed Forces to reclaim land and establish parking spaces in the capital city till he took over as Chief Minister in the year 2000. The construction of parking lots, particularly for vehicles from rural areas that visit Shillong everyday, was one of his pet projects. He managed to negotiate with the Defence Authorities to part with prime land at Luckier Road and Khlieh Ïew Duh (Bara Bazaar) to enable the projects to become a reality.

Reservation of Jobs in Central Government Establishments

In the year 1979, the Government was facilitating the acquisition of land for the establishment of a Research Station of the Indian Council of Agricultural Research (ICAR) in the state. The issue was raised in the Assembly by Prof Martin N Majaw and Mawlong. Prof Majaw urged the State Government to first plan and negotiate an employment policy with the Central Government so that the locals from Meghalaya and those from other North-Eastern states should get first preference for employment in its offices and

institutions. Majaw, who was extremely critical of the permission that was given to the ICAR even suggested that the 'departments which do not relate to Meghalaya should be shifted to other places of the North-East.' Mawlong's opinions didn't differ much from Majaw's.

Later in 1995, as an MLA in the Opposition, Mawlong expressed reservation about the establishment of a Central Agricultural University in Umiam Khwan on the same premises as Prof Majaw's. Retrieved records[39] reveal that there was an offer from the Central Government in the early 1990s to establish the university in Meghalaya. In her petition to SC Marak, the Chief Minister, Ivory Shylla, who was the President of the Mahila Morcha of Bharatiya Janata Party (BJP) inquired about the status. The Chief Minister blamed Mawlong for opposing the proposal as it was to be setup in Umïam, a village in Umroi constituency. Later, in a meeting, Mawlong acknowledged to Shylla that the project was stalled because he had raised objections and halted any move for land acquisition. Mawlong wanted a 'written assurance' from the Central Government to reserve at least a considerable number of jobs for the locals. However, neither did he receive any response nor did the State Government try to negotiate with the powers in Delhi. He expressed futility to grant

39 U Nongsaiñ Hima, 18 September 1996

any such permission to establish such institutions where most locals hardly get any employment and instead incur unnecessary loss of land. He cited the examples of Rangmen Cantonment, ICAR, and the North-East Space Application Centre—all Central Government offices established in his constituency itself, but most of the employees were non-indigenous as there was no proper employment policy to make it mandatory for such institutions to give meaningful employment to the locals.

In the year 1996, there was another offer. In a letter dated July 22, Chaturanan Mishra, the Union Minister of Agriculture, wrote a letter to Mawlong informing about the Central Government's intention to establish a College of Post-Graduate Studies, a constituent college of the Central Agricultural University at Umiam near the ICAR Complex. Proximity to the ICAR was cited by the Government as the primary reason for choosing the place. It was believed that this could be of much help to the proposed college. The Minister exhorted Mawlong to expedite the matter at the earliest, by convincing people to provide land and No-Objection Certificates from the authorities.

The matter was reported frequently by the vernacular dailies of Shillong but Mawlong categorically stated that he was not against the establishment of the college; nor did he unnecessarily prevent the establishment of the university in the earlier years. Instead, he wanted

clarity on the employment policy in black and white. He said in 1997[40] that 'the ICAR has not been able to achieve the desired results,' and as long as the Government's perspective on the matter was ambiguous, he would continue to oppose the establishment of such institutions that required extensive acres of land, but functioned on dubious policies and promised nothing much in return. As of March 2020, the University has two campuses in Ri Bhoi District, and it again made it to the floor of the Assembly for discussion where an opposition member alleged that the University had 'flouted' the rules related to employment as only 5% of the Scheduled Tribes got appointed in the University,[41] prompting the Chief Minister to assure an investigation into the matter.

In spite of his opposition to the University, Mawlong shared a congenial rapport with the officers and other staff. He supported the agitation by the Joint Action Committee, which included farmers, pressure groups, and the ICAR employees' association, to reinstate its Director, Dr S Laskar, after his unceremonious removal from the position. Being a frequent guest and Chief Adviser to the ICAR, Mawlong often exhorted the scientists to work conscientiously with the farmers and

40 U Nongsaiñ Hima, 18 September 1997

41 https://nenow.in/north-east-news/meghalaya/meghalaya-govt-to-pursue-with-centre-to-establish-central-agriculture-university-in-state.html

peasants, urging them to visit the fields instead of confining themselves to their laboratories.

Anti-Foreigners Movement

In 1975, the All Assam Students' Union (AASU) and the All Assam Gana Sangram Parishad (AAGSP) were leading large-scale agitations and demonstrations in the state of Assam to compel the Government of India to identify and expel illegal foreign immigrants to safeguard the political rights of the indigenous Assamese people. The demand sprung after the increase of the state's population in Assam by 31 per cent in the decade 1961-1971, whereas, the national average was 24 per cent. The increase was attributed to the illegal infiltration of foreign nationals from Bangladesh, a country with which the state shares almost a 500-km-long border. The threat of losing their identity to the so-called 'illegal migrants and foreigners' led to wide scale agitation and riots whose repercussions were felt in Meghalaya. Students and citizens, mobilised by the Tribal Women's Association (also called TWADAM) and the Khasi Students' Union (KSU), thronged the streets, demanding for identification and removal of the names of 'foreigners' from the state's electoral rolls. Houses were burnt, and many lost their lives. Such communal riots and tension escalated in the later years, particularly in 1987 and 1992. The Government was seen as adopting a partial attitude by rehabilitating the

non-indigenous people, turning a blind eye to the atrocities faced by the locals, particularly at the hands of the Central Reserve Police Force (CRPF). The opposition raised the matter in the State Assembly.

In the Budget Session of 1980, PR Kyndiah of the APHLC moved a resolution to take steps to ensure the names of foreign nationals were deleted from the electoral rolls of Meghalaya.

Mawlong, as member of the Opposition remarked that the issue had been agitating the minds of the members of the House to a great extent during the last few days.

> Judging from figures there is an abnormal increase of the (non-indigenous) population in our State, it really shows a sign of danger. Therefore, it is time to come up with certain proposals to check the increase of the foreign nationals and one of the steps to check the increase of foreign nationals is first to delete the names of these foreign nationals from the electoral rolls.

He worried that if they were not deleted, they would usurp the rights due to the Indian citizens.

Border Issue

Although Meghalaya was carved out of Assam in 1972, problems with its parent state still persist as the boundary between the two states has not been demarcated clearly. As of May 2020, more than one hundred cases of disputes occurred across the inter-state border with Assam between the years 2009 and 2020, ranging from harassment by Assam police personnel to raising of illegal construction.[42] The two states share a boundary that is over eight hundred kilometers long, covering almost all the major districts of Meghalaya, including Ri Bhoi. The villages that fall along the fringes of this inter-state boundary are often subjected to innumerable problems, including illegal land encroachment.

Mawlong frequently highlighted the problems of the people living in the disputed villages under his constituency, collectively called Block II, to draw attention of the Government. In the Budget Session in 1978, the year in which he won as an independent candidate from Umroi, he recounted an incident in the border area of Umroi.

> 'On the 2nd of July 1977, the Assam Police from the Karbi-Anglong District came to two villages of Jatalong and Sabuda and arrested three of our people. After the arrest they were harassed and beaten up and were taken to jail for about a week or more.'

Finally, they were found in Nowgong (Nagaon) Jail in Assam and were brought back with the

42 https://www.telegraphindia.com/north-east/meghalaya-lists-more-than-100-disputes-across-the-inter-state-border-with-assam/cid/1774825

help of the District Council authorities and other sources. Since the locals were from the 5 or 6 villages, which are in the border area, they had been facing hardship and were constantly living in fear of being harassed or arrested by the Assam authorities, added Mawlong. The locals also feared that the land they had cultivated for many years might also be taken away and given instead to those recognized by the Assam authorities.

During the 1978 elections, the villages of Ummat, Umlaper, Subada, and Jatalong that fell under Umroi constituency, had been considered or taken to be part and parcel of the Khasi Hills District. But the Assam Government tried to claim those villages, particularly the villages of Karbi-Anglong District, and also harassed the villagers. Mawlong was concerned that unless something was done from Meghalaya's side, people 'will not be able to stay in those villages and a time might come that these border people might be asked to vacate those lands'.

In 1989, after a visit with fellow MLA, Hopingstone Lyngdoh to Raid Nongtung which falls under the disputed areas of Block II, a discussion was initiated in the Assembly where Lyngdoh narrated the suffering of those residing in the area and the atrocities that they faced. The visit to Raid Nongtung was made by the duo after it was made known that from the Assam side, 'they have destroyed all the monuments, all the

sacred places which were used to perform rituals, by the Raij Nongtung.' Lyngdoh also alleged that the Forest Department of Assam had encroached into Meghalaya's territory and made plantations in those sacred places. He reasoned that those living on the Assam side had the audacity to commit such atrocities because even in the far-flung border villages, they had their security forces to protect their people, and they even escorted contractors who felled timber from Meghalaya's forests. The same was not the case with Meghalaya. Mawlong urged the Meghalaya Government to immediately take steps to post police force in the disputed areas 'to protect the people from harassment and also from our land being encroached upon by the Government of Assam.'

He also worried that it had been 16 years since the state was formed and yet the boundaries were not well defined. Had the leaders assured an agreement with the Assam Government or in the North-East Re-organisation Act, 1971, we would not be facing the issue now, he added.

The first sincere effort initiated by the heads of governments of the states was in 1985 when the Chandrachund Boundary Commission was constituted by Chief Minister Captain Williamson A Sangma and his counterpart Hiteswar Saikia. However, nothing much came out of that arrangement as Meghalaya objected to the recommendations made by the commission citing favouritism for the bigger

state, Assam. A concerted effort was initiated in 2000 and 2001, by the Chief Minister of Assam, Prafulla Kumar Mahanta and his counterpart, EK Mawlong to resolve the issue. The duo extensively toured and surveyed the border villages to understand the needs and aspirations of the people. The states had almost resolved the issue through a mutual understanding of 'give-and-take', but Mahanta's Government couldn't retain power in the general elections in 2001. The installation of a new Government in Assam buried the chance of solving the issue during Mawlong's tenure as Chief Minister.

Alternate Airport

Meghalaya at present has one functioning airport named The Shillong Airport, located at Umroi that has taken years to develop amidst multiple problems like inadequate land for expansion of the runway, long drawn protests against inadequate compensation to landowners, low visibility because of the presence of the hillocks in and around the airport leading to inability to land bigger Boeing aircrafts.

In the 80s, Vayudoot, which was a joint-venture between Indian Airlines and Air India, started its operations there but had to wind up subsequently due to lack of public response. Flights operated in fifty-seaters till Calcutta (Kolkata) only. In the year 1990, Mawlong had proposed an alternate site at Umwang, a village in the disputed Block II area and even visited the place with the Chief Minister, BB Lyngdoh. In 1994, he brought up the issue again in the Assembly and suggested that due to the reported unfeasibility of the airport at Umroi, a new site at Madan Umwang–a vast and beautiful area–could easily be converted into a Regional, National or International Airport. The new airport could cater to the immediate requirements of at least three districts: Jaiñtia Hills, Khasi Hills, and Karbi Anglong in Assam. During 1990-91, the then Chief Minister BB Lyngdoh and Mawlong visited New Delhi and proposed the new site to the Union Civil Aviation Ministry. But the matter could not be followed up as Lyngdoh's Government barely lasted for two years.

In the year 1995, Mawlong again proposed a Resolution in the Assembly 'to recommend to the Government of India for constructing an alternative and viable airport at Madan Umwang of Ri Bhoi District.' As the project involved huge financial implications, he cited an example from Karnataka where the State Government intended to hand over the construction of a rural airport to a 'consortium comprising Tata Industries Ltd (TIL), Raytheon (USA), Changi Airport Authority (Singapore), and Sembawang Corporation (Singapore)' on a joint-venture basis with the State Government. He proposed to constitute an expert committee comprising economic experts and even officials from the Government of Assam as the village

falls in the disputed area. He looked at it as an opportunity to perhaps address the boundary issue with the neighbouring state. While supporting the resolution, BB Lyngdoh acknowledged that the proposed site was 'a very central place for Assam and Meghalaya' and that had he been the representative of the area, he would have also proposed Madan Umwang as the site for a better airfield.

Farmers' Problems

Since Mawlong was familiar with farming practices as he had had first-hand experience in it as a young man, he understood the plight of the poor peasants. He often highlighted the various problems faced by them in the Assembly and even articulated novel ideas on how to ease their condition. In 1977, a devastating hail-storm in some areas under Ri Bhoi destroyed standing crops in many villages. Two years later, in 1979, a drought befell on the whole of Ri Bhoi Sub-Division. In the Winter Session the same year, he raised the issue of compensation to farmers affected by natural calamities. He said that about 486 villages were affected by the calamity and the Government also officially declared them drought-affected.

> 'But then, after many months of waiting for help of the Government, only in the month of August-September, a small help was given by the Government in the form of maize seeds to be distributed to the drought-affected families. ... At that time

> most of the people were happy about the distribution of maize but we were also told through the Gram Sevaks or the persons of the Blocks that this maize is not worth consuming because it is treated seed.'

He told the House that most villagers worried about using the treated maize as they could not consume it themselves or use it as feed for poultry or even sow it as the season was over by August-September.

In the year 1994, he proposed a resolution to establish Satellite Markets to help farmers sell their produce in smaller markets. This would also help reduce congestion from the city where there was only one main market, called Iewduh. He remarked that although the Honourable Governor of Meghalaya laid the foundation stone for a regulated market in 1990 at Mawiong, even four years later, there were no signs of its functioning.

> 'I do not know the reasons why it takes such a long time to construct a market by the Government agencies. Any way, we should have more markets in and around this capital city. For example, we can have one at Nongkrem side, one at Mawngap and the other at Marbisu side and one at Bhoi area like Umroi. Since there is no market in those areas, the people are facing problems especially when there is a bandh or strike in Shillong.'

About 80 per cent of the population in the state[43]

43 http://megagriculture.gov.in/PUBLIC/agri_scenario_introduction.aspx

are farmers engaged in tilling the earth to produce various agriculture and horticultural products including vegetables, spices and other crops. Mawlong stressed on the importance of supporting them and also discouraged *jhum* cultivation. Lauding the efforts of farmers for successfully growing new crops, he proposed a resolution in the Budget Session of 1995 to categorise Broomstick as an agricultural cash crop and not as a forest produce' . He explained that lately farmers had taken up Broom cultivation in a large way due to its profitability. But the Government was yet to recognise it as an agricultural crop and classified it as a forest produce. He urged the Government to recognise Broomstick as an agricultural cash crop so that some benefits could be extended to the farmers in case of any natural calamity as experienced in the past. Also, the District Councils were the sole collectors of royalty earned from the broomstick being a forest produce, thereby, rendering loss to the State Government. In the abandoned *jhum* fields, Broomstick cultivation could be encouraged in a big way so that the farming community at large would benefit from it.

Mawlong also advocated for other farmers' issues like regulating the price of crops, particularly ginger. Since ginger is a widely grown crop that

often fetches a good price, he reasoned that the middle men determined the cost price, making farmers completely dependent upon them.

Demanding Accountability in the Calcutta Meghalaya House Deal

In his address to the State Assembly in the Budget Session of the year 1990 the Governor of Meghalaya, Madhukar Dighe stated, 'The Government has decided to undertake reconstruction of buildings of the Meghalaya House at Calcutta for optimal utilisation of land and buildings and to generate additional resources for the State.' It is pertinent to note that subsequent governments had tried to address the question of demolishing the first Meghalaya House located at Russel Street in Kolkata due to its dilapidated condition. But demolishing the old structure without having an alternative would render it difficult for Meghalayans who travel to that city. As Minister of the General Administration Department (GAD) in 1990-91, Mawlong negotiated with the Government of West Bengal for an alternate site to construct a second Meghalaya House in the event of the first being demolished.

In the Budget Session in 1993, he reminded the House that land in Calcutta was purchased by the State of Meghalaya from the West Bengal Government at Rs 1.72 crores for the purpose of constructing the alternate Meghalaya House and

urged the Government of the day to be proactive in the matter:

> 'I met the Chief Minister, Jyoti Basu and we agreed to buy that land. So, I would request the Government to take up construction works and especially since the first Meghalaya House at Calcutta, according to reports received from the PWD is no longer safe. We have to demolish that house and build another and at the same time, build quarters at the available plot purchased in 1990-91.'

Three years later, he raised another query in the Budget Session of the year 1996 with regard to the progress of the construction of the new Meghalaya House, and criticised the Government for arbitrarily allotting the work to a private company saying,

> 'The Meghalaya House in Calcutta has been allotted to Peerless Developers. I would like to know whether any tender or quotation has been invited before we allotted to this company? And at what cost? Whether any estimates had been prepared. On what basis was it allotted to Peerless?'

On March 19, 1996, Mawlong again criticized the Government for its arbitrary decision on allotment of work for construction of the second Meghalaya House. 'I heard this is going to be awarded to Peerless for construction, because Peerless has been good to Meghalaya to give a loan of Rs17 crores. As a goodwill sign of gratitude, they will reward to Peerless Company.'

He asked whether any tender was floated, project reports made and competitions assessed before awarding to any company. He feared that in the absence of the same, the company would pay its chosen price and there would be no one to question it.

The Minister-in-Charge of GAD, Kitdor Syiem, in his reply to the queries related to the allotment of the work to the said company, stated in the Assembly on April 3, 1996 that no tender was floated because they thought since Peerless Developers was one of the premier construction agencies in Calcutta, giving them work was in the best interest of the state. Syiem added that another reason for giving Peerless Developers the work was that the state was facing financial problems in 1994-95 and Peerless had come to the rescue of the Government during that time and hence, giving them the work for Meghalaya House was thought as a 'good gesture.'

The incumbent Chief Minister Salseng C Marak also assured,

> The Government has decided to entrust the construction work to Peerless Construction Company Wing, Calcutta as per the MoU signed. So far, Peerless has not increased the cost of construction as pointed out by Mr Mawlong which he expressed his apprehension that the price

> might go up or may not comply with the contract agreement. The cost of the construction is at Rs 600 lakhs and they cannot go back from their commitment. There is no scope for them also to raise the amount.'

In his many years as an Opposition member in the Legislative Assembly, Mawlong highlighted issues he thought were integral to the development of the state. In fact, once a session was named after him, 'the EK Mawlong Session'. Former Legislator and Minister, Manas Chaudhuri in his obituary said,

> He dominated sessions so much on every aspect and he raised issues relevant to the State in a very very pointed manner. He made the ruling side's life a little more uncomfortable by his very strong and committed role in the House.

Fellow members in the treasury, including Chamberlain B Marak, often praised him for 'the fecundity of imagination and resourcefulness of ideas…(who is) unputdownable and unrelenting in so far as the rural priorities are concerned… He is known for his robust common sense, reasonableness and proven track record of parliamentary performances of a high order.'

EL Lyttan, former Secretary of the Legislative Assembly says that Mawlong was a proficient and eloquent Legislator who knew the subject matter well. He was always well-prepared and his

presence was felt by one and all, he added. What he remembers most is Mawlong's association and unique connection with the grass-root people, particularly of Umroi. To them, he always extended his help and support generously in the many years that he was their MLA, says Lyttan.

THE FATHER OF UMROI

Ar phew san snem la jop shi jop;	For twenty-five years he's been winning;
Ïeng skhem mynta, wat ym pyntlot.	Stand steady now, do not wither.
Ïeng skhem paitbah, shawei wat ju brai;	Stand firm people, don't look elsewhere;
Ban i'u Pa Nah nga dang lah u Pa Trai.	A stepdad isn't as good as a natal one.
Pa Nah u ong, 'u khunruit u leh kyrtong';	The uncle says, 'a nephew is contesting';
Pa Trai jong ngi dei i Bah EK Mawlong.	Our natal father is Bah EK Mawlong.
Peit ho paidbah, shawei wat ju brai;	Beware people, don't look elsewhere;
Ban i'u Pa Nah nga dang lah u Pa Trai.	A stepdad isn't as good as a natal one.

(Excerpt from a song sung by villagers of Raid Ïapngar in the 1998 Election Rally at Ïew Umroi).

EK MAWLONG'S association with the people of Umroi lasted more than thirty years as their representative in the State Assembly and District Council, except for one term in 2003. Many people recall him affectionately. Most attribute much of the development work in Umroi to Mawlong. Accounts of the kind of help he rendered in the construction of infrastructure, and to individuals in general are legendary.

Many believe that he had a knack of identifying capable local leaders at the village level. The leaders were mostly simple men and women with impeccable integrity, who tirelessly worked with him through the dust and grime of the elections, and when they tasted victory, the same leaders helped him in identifying the needs of individuals in the village. They were also his eyes and ears who would update him with relevant information, including the counter moves of political rivals. If a family was in need of any help, his supporters encouraged them to seek Mawlong's help. His house at Lumsohphoh, Lower Mawprem in Shillong was accessible to most of his constituents. His people were welcome at his house at any hour but mornings were typically the busiest.

Often, visitors to the city missed their buses to return, and since vehicles were scarce, they would spend the night at Mawlong's house. The ones who wanted to explore the city would spend an extra night or more and Mawlong would never refuse. Many who were seeking treatment for their family in Shillong sought help from him, especially if their relatives passed away or they ran short of money.

For such visits, Mawlong had prepared a separate

room in the basement with a few beds and blankets. Whenever any family member complained of such intrusions, he would gently remind them with a smile, 'We are what we are because of the people of Umroi. We should respect them.'

The people of Umroi returned the same affection and regard, particularly because of his down-to-earth approach, easy access, patience and dynamic yet gentle leadership skills. He had ample patience to explain his ideas and Government policies to villagers who were less educated. The villages were divided into units and the units were further clustered together into areas. Many villagers were made leaders of small and big units who later decided on the schemes for their villages as part of Umroi's Development Committee. The Development Committee worked hand-in-hand with the *durbar shnong*[44] to decide on the nature of the schemes that the villages needed in a particular financial year.

On any trip to Umroi in his Ambassador or jeep, he made it a point to stop and ferry people in his vehicle whenever he saw a familiar face walking along the road. On visits to villages, he would carry two or three packets of sweets for children.

***

44 A traditional village institution of the Khasis which comprises all Khasi inhabitants of not less than 18 years of age of a village, where the prevailing age-old customary and traditional governance and adjudication are carried out.

In his run as a public representative of Umroi, Mawlong was elected as a candidate of the Hill State People's Democratic Party (HSPDP) on four occasions—thrice as MLA in 1983, 1988, and 1993, and once as MDC in 1989. In 1998, he contested and won as a candidate of the United Democratic Party (UDP), but lost in 2003. In 2008, he was re-elected on a UDP ticket.

His principal adversaries in Umroi were normally candidates put up by the Indian National Congress (INC). The most formidable of all was Fleming Stone Lapang, a native of Bhoirymbong village, whom he contested against in the elections from 1978 to 1993. Lapang, a respectable school teacher of Myngken Presbyterian High School in Bhoirymbong, had a strong support base and considerable vote bank, but Mawlong always had the better of him.

One of the early supporters and local leaders who Mawlong identified in the late 1970s was Dwikshon Kharkongor from Umtung village. He was Mawlong's confidant and trusted aide, whose friendship transcended the entrapments of formality.

Currently in his 70s, the lanky man who is fondly called Babu Dwik, likes to chew betel nut that he pounds with his sturdy hands in a wooden mortar that never leaves his side. From Sohryngkham village in East Khasi Hills District, the St Anthony's School and College product still

sports his signature salt and pepper hair that hasn't changed for as long as people can remember.

> Whenever Bah Heh and I would meet anywhere in a large group, like a meeting of some kind, we never shook hands. Cordial as he was, he'd extend his hand to one and all. But I never shook his hand. If you meet any member of your family, do you shake hands?

Since Babu Dwik was a teacher at the same school as Fleming Stone Lapang, he supported his colleague in the 1978 election. After the culmination of the election, Mawlong approached Babu Dwik to join his group to work together in subsequent elections and to help him in the overall planning of development work in the constituency.

When Mawlong first approached Babu Dwik to support him immediately after the February 1978 election, he declined, saying that it would look bad to desert Lapang. However, Mawlong was persistent and visited Babu Dwik's house on some pretext or the other.

> I don't know, and I never asked why he kept insisting so much at that time. But later I realised that it was his signature style. The more people tried to turn him away, the more he tried to win their support in his own way. It must have been in his fifth or sixth visit that I relented and we sat down to chalk out a map for the future.

That was the birth of their association, which

lasted till the very end. Whenever Mawlong would visit Babu Dwik's house after that, he would head straight into the kitchen, and behave like any member of the family, says Babu Dwik.

> And it was not a pretentious show of affection; that was his nature. Also, his kind-heartedness, patience and benevolence endeared everyone towards him. And because he was so free with all of us, we felt the same way for him and his family. His house was like our house.

During these visits, Mawlong noticed that the teacher had a huge family to support on a meagre income.

> So slowly he introduced me to a different world of department contract works and started augmenting minor construction work in the Public Health Engineering (PHE) Department. Alongside these works, we worked tirelessly to strengthen his support among the people.

Together they visited many villages to understand the needs of the people, and identified village leaders who could work for the welfare of their people. He brought huge development in infrastructure to the constituency and Babu Dwik says that it was possible 'because of his rapport with the officers of the various departments like education, health, irrigation, Public Works Department (PWD), and PHE.'

> Once we had to identify the catchment area for potable water supply to Nongtraw village. The tall and bulky Mr Borthakur (from the PHE department) huffed and puffed his way up the steep forested hills. And when the work was done, we all sat together to share a common meal. A surprised Mr Borthakur remarked that it was the first time he saw an MLA squat on the ground to share a meal with those who were subordinate to him.

When Babu Dwik realised that the responsibilities Mawlong gave him made it difficult to do justice to the school, he resigned in 1979 to continue doing the work facilitated by him.

The people of Umroi constituency, although simple and unassuming can't be fooled easily as most voters are politically conscious and hence, demand accountability from their representatives. In markets and popular tea stalls, politics is usually the topic of discussion. Since the formation of the state, the constituency has always had two major political factions: the Congress and the regional parties.

In fact, in the first two elections, rival candidates used the outsider issue to weaken his stronghold over his constituency. Chosterfield Khongwir recounted that initially Mawlong had to struggle to gain a strong foothold, particularly after the bifurcation of Umroi constituency.

In 1972, the constituency was very vast. Bah Heh Kek's native place Mawmih, which is now under Sohiong constituency, was then a part of Umroi. Post-1972, Mawmih and its adjoining villages were bifurcated and were no longer included under Umroi. So what remained of the familiar territory to him was Mawlyndep, Umraleng, Umbir and Niangdai areas.

Post-bifurcation, most of the villagers under Umroi, including Bhoirymbong and beyond, considered Mawlong an 'outsider' or a non-local who did not belong to the Bhoi sub-tribe. Many opponents would spread such fears to create confusion in the minds of the voters.

Slowly, most started to welcome them. Khongwir would clarify in public meetings that Mawlong was an honest and diligent man. He would instead ask how can he be an outsider if he is the son of the beloved state, and an elected MDC of Umroi?

Even Proi Sohtun, a staunch Congressman and a prominent personality of Bhoirymbong village, admired Mawlong for his rapport with his voters. Sohtun's parents had died when he was very young and did whatever job he could, including as a cow and goat herdsman. Politics always interested him and when the opportunity arrived, he campaigned hard for the Congress. He remembers carrying enormous baskets full of buns on his back from one polling station to another so that the supporters could have the buns with a cup of tea.

> But no matter how hard we tried, it was difficult to defeat Bah Mawlong. He had his own tactics. Yet in every election we fought with the hope that we'd win. It was only in 1993 that Bah FS Lapang was in touching distance of a victory, but that too didn't turn out well.

Eventually, Sohtun had the opportunity to work with a Congress MLA in 2003 when Mawlong was defeated. It took a lot of effort to defeat Mawlong as he had a wonderful connection with the voters, particularly those who were financially weak. Mawlong's supporters, Sohtun recalls, supported him with all their heart and soul.

> Whenever there was a meeting that he organised somewhere, men and women, old and young, would climb onto any vehicle that they could get, be it an open truck or a jeep trailer. They'd dance away to glory, chanting his name. I witnessed such scenes with my own eyes.

Sohtun adds that the one thing he most appreciated about Mawlong was his fairness. Typically, representatives used their influence to stop rivals from getting contracts in various departments. Sohtun says that Mawlong never resorted to such tactics even though he could have with his network.

In the 1970s, when he was Member of the District Council (1972) and later as Member of the Legislative Assembly (1978), Mawlong had become familiar with the problems and prospects of the

constituency and his support base had also grown. One of his most ardent supporters was Frederick Allan Wahlang, a resident of Umroi Laban Saro, who was also its Rangbah Shnong or Headman. Late Wahlang's wife, Magrisha Syiem, who witnessed the two brainstorm and relentlessly work for the Umroi Pyllun area, recalled the early days when Mawlong was MDC. He entrusted her husband, a pragmatic and educated man, with 'the task of convincing villagers to cooperate with the Government and its officials; to part with land, if required, for road expansion, schools, and water reservoirs.'

The cooperation of the people was necessary as the land tenure in Meghalaya made any important development work difficult without their assent and understanding. Land is either individually owned or owned by the clans. Some lands are also under the village or the *Shnong,*[45] cluster of villages or *Raid*[46] or traditional Khasi kingdoms known as *Hima*[47]. Since Wahlang was an educated *Rangbah Shnong*[48] and originally from Laitumkhrah in Shillong but settled in Umroi, Mawlong understood that delegating the task of convincing villagers to Wahlang could ensure smooth implementation of the plans he had in mind. The setting up of most schools, construction of arterial roads and water supply in the Umroi area can

45 Village
46 Cluster of villages
47 Traditional states within the Khasi Hills
48 Village Head

be attributed to both of them.

Like Wahlang and his family, many others from various hamlets of Umroi across Kyrdem Kulai, Lasharai (Mawleiñ-Mawkhan), Umbir, Mawlyndep, Umiam, and other villages helped Mawlong during the initial days and remained loyal to him during his long tenure as MLA. Two of them were from the nearby villages of the disputed Block II area, Miwell Shadap and Ser Syiemiong.

Syiemïong was one of his foot soldiers in the Mawlasnai area. Famous for placing bets with rivals during the election season, many remember him breaking into a spontaneous dance in the middle of Bhoirymbong market when Mawlong won his fourth consecutive election. A small-time businessman, he had the pulse of the people on the ground and could win friends by his wit and humourous stories. A frequent visitor to Mawlong's house, he would offer help to those facing difficulty and never expected anything in return. Syiemïong recalled a memorable incident that happened sometime before 1996 when large-scale felling and sale of timber was still legal in Meghalaya. Being a timber dealer, Syiemïong was chopping down trees in the forests of Mawlasnai when, unknowingly, he cut down timber from another forest that belonged to a different owner. The owner of that forest was furious when he learnt about it, so he filed a complaint at Umïam Police Outpost against Syiemïong. The police were in pursuit of the clueless

Syiemïong who was busy chopping down more trees. He was finally arrested in Shillong when the complainant saw him in Ïewduh. Syiemïong was so embarrassed that he requested the policeman not to handcuff him.

The policeman obliged but took him straight to the Court of the District Council which sentenced him to prison after depositing a surety of Rs 30,000. In the Shillong District Jail, Syiemïong met people who had committed other more grievous crimes. He was really depressed and upset. At about ten o'clock at night though, he was almost in tears because of relief and happiness. As he held on to the bars of the cell, sticking his nose between the cell bars trying to get some fresh air because of the foul smell, he saw Mawlong from a corner of his eye.

Mawlong was holding something in his hand and enquiring about Syiemïong from the prison authorities. Syiemïong screamed out to him, 'Bah Heh! Bah Heh!' When Mawlong finally saw Syiemïong, he grinned with amusement. In his hand was a tiffin with warm, home-cooked food. Looking at Syiemïong he laughed light-heartedly, and consolingly said, 'This is not such an awful place to stay for some time, Ser. Even I had spent a night here along with Martin Majaw[49]. Have this food while it's warm. I will bring one lawyer tomorrow

49 Mawlong, Prof Martin Narayan Majaw and other political leaders were arrested for protesting against the Land Reform Bill in 1978.

and you will be out in no time.' Syiemïong relished the food, sharing it with the strangers in the cell. When Syiemïong told the inmates who the food delivery man was, they were all so surprised. The next day Mawlong came with one lawyer and got Syiemïong out of there. He also ensured that he got back the surety amount.

That was not the only time Syiemïong got into trouble. On another occasion at Jeep Stand in Ïewduh, he accidently hit the handyman of the second-hand bus which he had bought and was trying his hand at driving. Syiemïong was reversing the bus to park it properly, but due to his inadequate height, he couldn't control the vehicle efficiently. So the handyman, who was a teenager, got squeezed between the bus and a wall. The impact punctured his abdomen, and he was grievously injured. A furious crowd gathered to help the boy; fortunately, the police arrived just in time before they could lynch Syiemïong. The furious policemen took Syiemïong to Civil Hospital for a medical check-up. They wanted to confirm whether he had taken alcohol. Syiemïong kept pleading that his foot couldn't reach the brakes on time, but they paid no heed to his pleas. Syiemïong assumed that he would rot in the stinking jail forever when he heard that the boy's intestines were seen dangling out of his stomach. Fortunately, before they could take him to the jail, Mawlong turned up at the hospital. Syiemïong recalls with

much fondness, 'He somehow negotiated with the doctors and the police and whisked me away from there to his office. That was my Bah Heh. Which MLA will visit you in jail with home-cooked food at ten o'clock at night?'

Miwell Shadap is another prominent leader in the disputed Block II. Mawlong and Shadap had known each other since Mawlong's MDC years. Shadap recalls how Mawlong acquainted himself with the ground realities and the tremendous problems the people were facing as a result of the unresolved border demarcation issue with Assam. Right from the 1960s onwards, the Khasi people of the area had many altercations with the non-Khasi residents, who were predominantly from the Nepali community. The Khasis were into agriculture and the Nepali people, known as *khuttiwala,*[50] reared cows and buffaloes. Whenever their animals strayed onto the fields of the Khasis devouring the plantations, it would lead to a conflict.

Another cause of frequent conflict was the fight to take control over the taxation at the local market at Madan Umwang. Assam had already set up police outposts at disputed areas, but the only police outpost on the Meghalaya side was one in Mawlasnai, which was ill-equipped and lacked adequate personnel. Thus, the people residing on the Assam side of the border had a distinct

50 People involved in animal husbandry

advantage. The locals alleged that the Assam police would often intimidate and even arrest the Khasi people residing there. The Khasis, who worked in their fields during the day and were fond of hunting at night, were often arrested for trespassing into the disputed forests, and for carrying weapons that were used for hunting. Mawlong would frequently negotiate with the Assam authorities for their release. In fact, many remember one such event that took place in the early 1980s.

Despite the hardships, the people's appeal to the Government, and Mawlong's strenuous pleas in the State Assembly to improve infrastructure in the border villages, it went unheeded for many years. Fed up with the apathy, he organised a memorable event where he gathered the men and women of the area to construct a *kuccha* road from Khyndewso village to Sabuda village, which was about 800 metres long. For two days, Mawlong, along with Prof Chosterfield and hundreds of villagers, dug the road together. After the work was done, there was a sumptuous traditional meal organised by Mawlong. Soon, the Public Works Department of the state took notice and constructed a bridge at Umtyngkong to connect it to Sabuda village.

In the year 1990, when Mawlong, along with the Chief Minister BB Lyngdoh, visited Madan Umwang to select the site for an alternative airport, there were consequences after they left the place. Miwell Shadap narrated that after the Chief

Minister's visit to Madan Umwang, the authorities in Assam were peeved because they claimed that the area belonged to them. They got to know that Shadap along with other local leaders were in the forefront along with the Chief Minister and Mawlong. So the Assam forces went looking for them on a Sunday when a big Church service was going on. They fled for their lives and hid inside a haystack that people had collected after the year's harvest. That was how he escaped impending arrest.

Shadap, like many others in the village, experienced first-hand the hardship of staying in the border villages. He recalls how efforts were made by both the governments of Assam and Meghalaya in resolving the issue when they constituted the Chandrachud Committee. Mawlong had taken Shadap and other leaders to Shillong with a representation to meet the Chairman and members of the committee. There were representations from villagers of other districts as well. But eventually the Chandrachud Committee's recommendations were rejected by Meghalaya as it allegedly favoured Assam. Later, during Mawlong's tenure as Chief Minister, he took up the border issue with Assam Chief Minister, Prafulla Kumar Mahanta. At that time, he wanted to land in a helicopter at Madan Umwang along with Mahanta but Shadap opposed this plan because of what had happened in 1990. Shadap told him that once he left, the Assam police would definitely arrest them. There was a minor

argument between the two regarding that issue, but Mawlong later relented.

Mawlong called Shadap regularly at public meetings across Umroi constituency as he was a good orator. Earlier, Shadap was staying in a village called Umtlih, which had poor connectivity by road. Mawlong would make sure that whenever there was a meeting anywhere, a vehicle was sent to pick and drop Shadap. Then Shadap told Mawlong that since they will be working together for many years, it would be best for him to shift to Umpohwin village, where Shadap knew a plot of land was available for Rs 8,000. Due to their long association, Mawlong provided the money to get that plot. Another time, when Shadap was out of funds to pay for his wife's treatment in Woodland Hospital in Shillong, he rushed to Mawlong's house at Lower Mawprem to explain his plight. Mawlong was not in a position to help but called an engineer posted at Umsning who came to his rescue.

> He asked the engineer if they had any pending bills that the department was yet to pay to me. The engineer replied in the affirmative and Bah Heh requested him to lend Rs 30,000 to me, and to adjust the amount later whenever the department could pay my pending dues…There are many other stories of the help he extended to me and others.

The border areas of Block II were not the only areas of conflict where Mawlong had to intervene.

In 1979-80, a very unusual but memorable event occurred when Mawlong himself had to take over as *Rangbah Shnong* of Mawbseiñ village. Following the communal riots in 1979 in Shillong, the non-indigenous communities in most places in the Khasi-Jaiñtia hills fled the state forsaking their homes and land. A particular community in Mawbseiñ escaped too leaving behind huge plots of land. Later, a dispute between two indigenous groups arose in the village as they fought for the ownership over a vacant piece of land. A violent confrontation between the groups ensued. A few lost their lives too. As MLA of the area, Mawlong intervened and even stayed in the village for many weeks. The police left nothing to chance and stationed in the village until near normalcy was restored. As one of the warring groups was led by the incumbent *Rangbah Shnong*, those who weren't in his support no longer trusted his leadership. After weeks of dialogue, the villagers resolved that until complete normalcy was restored, Mawlong was to take over as their village head. He obliged. For over a year he was the *Rangbah Shnong* of Mawbseiñ village, and with time the goodwill among the people was restored.

With regard to development work in the constituency, Babu Dwikshon Kharkongor, who was Chairman of the Block Development Committee, for a long period and was well acquainted with the various schemes that were implemented in Umroi says:

> I can well and truly say that before the MLA schemes were launched and implemented in 1991, bringing rapid development to the constituency was difficult for Bah Heh Kek. There were only Department Schemes which were implemented by the Block, and due to the meagre amount, not much development work could be done. After the implementation of the Special Rural Works Programme (SRWP) and the Community Rural Roads Programme (CRRP) in the year 1991 though, community participation in the development works became more visible.

At the time when the schemes were implemented, the amount allotted to each constituency was a meagre Rs 6 lakh. Today, the figure is at Rs 2.5 crore. Like most other legislators, Mawlong supported various resolutions to increase the allotment to the SRWP and CRRP as he felt that the onus was upon the individual MLA to get community assets like school buildings, community halls, foot bridges and road schemes. In the Budget Session of 1995, he said:

> With the implementation of such schemes right from 1991 during the MUPP Government, we found that the public representative has become more responsible because this scheme is channelised through the MLA, and if not properly implemented, the MLA concerned will be responsible. Therefore, it is good that more responsibility is being given to the

> MLAs so that they can supervise other schemes as well as the Block Community Development schemes and any other schemes implemented by the Government.

Babu Dwik says that most roads, Government schools, Public Health Centres, Community Health Centres, potable water, and electricity connection in the Umroi constituency were ensured thanks to Mawlong's contribution.

> Notwithstanding whether an individual or a village supported him or not, he distributed schemes equally to the entire constituency. I can confidently say that 90 percent of all Public Health Engineering (PHE) schemes that we have today were his handiwork.

He adds that most roads that connect Umroi from far away Kyrdem Kulai till Mawlasnai–a distance of almost 50 km–were either constructed during his time or initiated by Mawlong. Dwikshon was closely associated with the Umsning Block and worked with various departments under Mawlong's guidance for years. He talks about Kyrdem village, which was a polling station with over 500 voters in the 1980s and 1990s.

> …whenever votes were counted during elections, Bah Heh would hardly get forty to fifty votes. But if you visit the village, you will find all the requirements that the people need: roads, schools, a Public

Health Centre, an Inspection Bungalow, and other infrastructure.

Among the many schemes attributed to him were water supply schemes at Mawlyndep, Umket, Pynthor, Lapudui, among many other villages; weaving workshop at Iapngar village; schools at Nongtraw, Umtangling, and several villages; and among innumerable road projects, most important was the road linkage from Lad Umroi-Mawlasnai to Diphu in Assam with financial assistance from the North Eastern Council. Based on accounts of the constituents, particularly those who worked closely with him through the *Dorbar Shnong*[51] and other development committees, they attribute most of the internal roads, water supply schemes and electricity connections to Mawlong's hard work and dedication. Bishar Dhar of Bhoirymbong village, and son of T Marbaniang, a close associate of Mawlong, says:

> I can confidently vouch for the fact that almost all the water supply schemes, roads, electricity, Government schools, durbar halls, community centres, the Bhoirymbong CHC, Kyrdem PHC, and many others in the constituency were all done during Bah Heh's time.'

Dhar says that there are many reports of

51 elected village council

Mawlong 'inaugurating school buildings, durbar halls, bridges, roads, water sources, or laying foundation stones for new projects.'

In Byrwa or Kyrdem Kulai areas, which were under the Umroi constituency during his tenure as MLA, most roads that he implemented through the state and central schemes are functional till this day. Locals from those areas fondly remember him for these and many other projects, adds Dhar.

Life in villages was not easy as they lacked basic facilities and communication was also poor, unlike today. As a representative of a rural constituency, trying to bring infrastructure development in a state with inadequate resources was always a tough task. Meril Warjri of Umraleng village which was under Umroi constituency, recalled the various schemes and benefits that her village and the adjoining hamlets received from Mawlong. In 1978, he inaugurated a school in Umraleng. During his tenure as MLA, most villages like Umbir, Mawlyndep, Mairung, Niangdai, Umniuh always voted for Mawlong as he ensured not just a road from Mawlyndep to Umraleng, but also electricity and water connections, toilets, rural housing, veterinary hospital, vegetable seeds and football grounds.

> I remember the water source identified for our village was located in Umriang village and the particular plot belonged to the Mawlong clan. Due to some internal rivalry, a section of the clan did not want

> to give permission to the PHE to draw water from there.

However, being an elder of the clan, Mawlong went with the PHE officers to measure the diameter of the source. That's how Umraleng got access to water. The adjoining villages, including Mawlyndep, Umbir, Usaw, Umniuh also got lucky due to his influence over the Thangkhiew clan, says Meril Warjri.

> The clan owns a lot of property, and their plot in the Umpanai village is the source of water supply to these four villages. And that too was possible because his paternal relations (the Thangkhiew clan) had a lot of respect for him. They readily permitted to draw water from the source located within their plot.

There are many stories about Mawlong from these villages. It is said that most locals had not seen a JCB until Mawlong sought help from Honsen Lyngdoh Mawphlang, a renowned contractor, to level the football grounds in Umraleng and Mawlyndep. Mawlong also helped the Mawlyndep village reclaim a portion of land from the Union Christian College in 1986-87 that was under dispute due to some flaws in the demarcation. The villagers and college were set to take the matter to court but Mawlong intervened and helped them reach an out-of-court settlement. The college returned a considerable portion of land to the

village, which had been so far under the possession of the college. Meril Warjri says:

> As a token of respect and gratitude, the village heads of that time Bah K Nongneng, Bah Phillip Kharpan, and Bah Kidren Mawlong went to meet Ma Heh Kek in his house at Lower Mawprem with a gift–an offer to choose any plot of land at Mawlyndep. But they were disappointed because he refused.

Shelina Nongbri of Bhoirymbong village, recalled a particular incident distinctly when Mawlong helped a distressed family complete the funeral rites of a deceased member. It was in the 1990s, when one of Nongbri's relatives passed away in Ganesh Das Hospital in Shillong. When news of her death reached the village, there were objections from several people with regard to the provision of giving her a burial ground, for reasons which Nongbri couldn't recall. As relatives, they didn't know what to do, and along with one cousin, Nongbri decided to dash to the hospital first. When they reached there, the authorities instructed them to take away her body, but they couldn't do so immediately because of the hostility at the village. Having no other option, they went to Mawlong's house at Lower Mawprem when it was already about six in the evening. He wasn't at home, and they were asked to stay over at his place that night. When Mawlong returned, it was

almost ten, and immediately inquired what the problem was. When they told him about the issue, he decided to accompany them to the hospital the next day. At the hospital, Mawlong met the doctor concerned and together went to see the woman. Surprisingly, she appeared to have come back to life. As she was a Catholic, Mawlong called a priest from Mawlai Parish to visit the hospital and confer the last rites to her. The priest readily obliged and after the last rites were done, the doctor declared that the woman had finally passed away. Later, Mawlong requested the same priest to provide some space at the Mawlai cemetery for a proper burial of the woman. Along with the two women, Mawlong attended the funeral and completed the rites quietly.

Like Nongbri's, there are innumerable personal stories of the kind of help the people received from Mawlong in his many years of association with them. In the year 1998, Mawlong told locals in a public rally how much affection he had received from them. Once during a meeting, an old lady was unable to shake hands with him but was still able to touch his coat.

> Someone told me that he saw her kissing the hand which touched my coat again and again. That is the affection and love that you have for me. The old and infirm come to me only with love. And I give my all in your service with dedication and heart full

of love and gratitude for everything that you have given me.

He also spoke candidly about the difficulties of being in public life. When someone who is ill gets admitted in a hospital in Shillong, they expect him to visit.

> If I don't visit them, they get annoyed. At times, when I'm in my vehicle and inadvertently don't wave at a supporter or friend, they stop talking to me and say, 'O Bah Heh doesn't need me anymore.'

He also acknowledged his connection with the people of Umroi. Despite the criticism from opponents, he believed that it was their job to criticise, but that no matter how 'big or small' his contribution, the people 'knew very well.'

> I have always believed that roads are the backbone of development; when we give people roads, they'll find their own ways toward earning a livelihood. When I came to this area in 1972-73 there was nothing; thick forests everywhere.

He pointed that Bhoirymbong looked no less than Shillong's Jeep Stand.[52] People, he said, 'made the most of the roads that have been provided to them.' One of his initiatives that stand testimony till today is the setting up of the SOS Village (Save Our Souls Village) in the constituency. The non-

52 A busy commercial area near Iewduh (Bara Bazaar) in Shillong

governmental organisation SOS caters to various child care programmes. His detractors accused him of indulging in corruption over the issue, perhaps because they were unsure what the objective of the project was. He said:

> I am happy to inform that the SOS—Save Our Souls Village—will soon come up at Umïam. For this also they (political opponents) accuse me of wrongdoing. Who will stay in that SOS village? They will all be children—Khasi, Jaiñtia, and Garo—who are orphans. How is it possible to be corrupt in such a project?

Mawlong always put the concerns of his people before his own. The people from Umroi would sing and dance to various songs composed by a singer ES Iawram from Pynursla village in East Khasi Hills, who often accompanied Mawlong during electoral campaigns, one of which perhaps sums up his dedication to his work and the people:

Ki ong namar jong phi, o i kloi ban tur shaphrang,
O kam pher wat la da hap u ryndang.
(For your sake, people say, he is always ready to march forward,
He wouldn't care even if he loses his life in the process.)

UPS AND DOWNS

IN THE quarter-century after the formation of the State, Meghalaya saw as many as twenty-two governments in ten tenures of the Legislative Assembly, of which fifteen had the INC at the helm. The dominance of the INC in the state has been attributed partly to the mushrooming of many regional political parties, their disunity, and many political defections that were effected until the implementation of the Anti-Defection Law in 1985. The law too had its loopholes as MLAs could defect and split from a party if they had sufficient numbers. And this was taken advantage of by most legislators to destabilise governments.

The post-1993 general election phase was a crucial one for the regional political parties of the state. Capt Sangma of the Congress had smoothly sailed through as Chief Minister in the third state Legislative Assembly (1983-88), during which Mawlong was the Speaker of the House. In the

fourth Assembly (1988-93), there was immense political instability; Purno A Sangma's Government lasted for about two years before he was replaced by BB Lyngdoh of the Hill People's Union (HPU). It was during the HPU-led Meghalaya United Parliamentary Party (MUPP) Government that Mawlong was made Minister of General Administration Department, Parliamentary Affairs and Law. That Government lasted for just a little more than a year from 26 March 1990 to 10 October 1991, after which President's rule was imposed for the first time in the history of the state.

On 7 August 1991, during the trial of strength in the Assembly, Speaker PR Kyndiah suspended the voting rights of five legislators—Monendro A Sangma, Miriam D Shira, Chamberlain B Marak, Simon Siangshai and Dr Donkupar Roy—acting on a complaint filed by the Congress' Hispreaching Son Shylla. All the five were independent legislators and the complaint was that three had joined the HSPDP and two the HPU, thus acting in contravention to the rules of the Tenth Schedule. When the Speaker pronounced his ruling to suspend the five, there was pandemonium in the House. Members of the ruling side climbed atop tables and stormed into the well of the Assembly, prompting the Speaker to adjourn the session. However, ten days later, the Speaker disqualified all the five members of the Assembly leading to the dismissal of the Government. The Governor,

Madhuram Dighe, decided not to invite any other party to form the Government and instead recommended imposition of President's Rule.

After President's Rule was revoked on 5 February 1992, DD Lapang of the INC took over as Chief Minister till February 1993 before elections to the Assembly were held that year. During Lapang's term, there were incidences of ethnic violence between the Khasis and Biharis that escalated in October 1992. The regional parties capitalised on the waning popularity of the Chief Minister, and Mawlong, who was then the HSPDP candidate from Umroi, ardently supported Constantine Lyngdoh of the HSPDP who had contested against Lapang from Nongpoh.

The acrimony between the regional parties and the Congress spilled over to the campaign for the 1993 General Election to the Legislative Assembly. Umroi and Nongpoh fall under Ri Bhoi district, and a representative of either constituency does have considerable influence over both the areas. EK Mawlong went all out against the incumbent Chief Minister and sitting Legislator of Nongpoh, DD Lapang, in that particular election, to the extent of abandoning the campaign in his own constituency, Umroi. In Umroi, he depended enormously on his local leaders to campaign for him in most of the villages.

In a recorded speech towards the end of the 1993 election campaign at a massive rally at Umroi Nongrah village, Mawlong first apologised to the

huge crowd and his supporters for not visiting all the villages over the election campaign period. '*Nga la ïohi ba ki nongïalam ki jong nga ki la tyrkhong raw-raw* (I have noticed that my leaders here have all become dry and shrivelled).' In his absence, amidst many difficulties, the local leaders worked hard to campaign for him. He reminded the people that they shouldn't be disheartened if he could not campaign in their village because in the 10-15 years as their representative, he had visited each and every village, and was well-acquainted with all the problems.

> So it shouldn't matter much that I have not visited all villages in these weeks leading to the election on February 15. I promise that those villages that I haven't visited during this election campaign, will be the first ones that I will step foot on after you renew your mandate and make me your MLA once again.

He apologised for not being able to provide proper vehicles to the attendees and many were left behind in the villages as transportation was insufficient. 'Most of you have come on foot; those who've come in vehicles, you yourselves have spent on fuel to get here,' he said. With an aim to defeat his nearest rival from the Congress, Flemingstone Lapang, he highlighted the desperation of the rivals but vowed not to reply in the same language.

> They know that they are losing from Umroi, so what are they doing now? They are tearing our posters, they burnt our HSPDP flag, they pelted stones at our leaders, and even beat them up. But I would like to tell you, do not be afraid because we are winning. We will win people's trust with love; we will win with perseverance; we will win with patience. Do not indulge in violence because after the acrimony of this election is over, our lives will return to normalcy and all of us have to live as one.

He reminded the voters that in that year, the three regional parties—Hill People's Union (HPU), Public Demands Implementation Committee (PDIC), and the Hill State People's Democratic Party (HSPDP)—though contesting separately as individual parties, were all under the same umbrella known as the Meghalaya Federation. He said that in all constituencies, voters supporting any of the three parties could vote for any such candidate, thus extending their support to the Meghalaya Federation, 'If you have friends in other constituencies, tell them to vote for the candidates contesting from any of the three parties. Ha U Sing! (On the symbol of the Lion!).'

The Meghalaya Federation was a unified political entity of the three main regional parties of the 1990s-the HPU, HSPDP and the PDIC, whose aim was to curtail the influence of the

Congress, particularly in the Khasi-Jaiñtia Hills. The parties realised that their separate existence was fragmenting the regional votes, and by coming together under one banner, they wanted to consolidate the support. The 1993 election was by far the most acrimonious of all elections at least in Umroi, with reports of stone pelting and assault, particularly in Bhoirymbong. The violence escalated after the declaration of results, when EK Mawlong polled 7,958 votes and the runner-up, Bah Fleming Stone Lapang of the Congress polled 7,072 votes. The houses of Dwikshon Kharkongor at Umtung village, T Marbaniang at Bhoirymbong, and many others who were the foremost supporters of Mawlong were stoned. The damage to the houses was extensive and fearing that the perpetrators would return, the family of Dwikshon Kharkongor fled to Mawlong's residence and stayed there for over two weeks.

In Nongpoh, the constituency where Mawlong had campaigned rigorously, Constantine Lyngdoh of the HSPDP got 7,474 votes whereas the incumbent Chief Minister, DD Lapang of the INC polled 6,379 votes. It was the first and only defeat for DD Lapang, a distinguished political personality, who had held the post of Chief Minister and was Minister on multiple occasions. Had he not lost his Nongpoh seat to Constantine Lyngdoh, he would have perhaps been elected as the Chief Minister, as the INC again went on to form the Government

for the next five years. The INC had won twenty-four seats in the 60-member House, and it could muster enough numbers largely due to the betrayal of a few elected MLAs of the HSPDP who split from the party and joined hands with the Congress. Mawlong, who was then the General Secretary of the HSPDP, was dejected as he had to again occupy the Opposition bench. He was livid as people from his own party had split and joined hands with the Congress. Due to these frequent defections and splits in the regional parties, the leaders led by EK Mawlong, Prof GG Swell, BB Lyngdoh, Sanbor Swell Lyngdoh and a host of others felt the growing need to come together into a single fold to be able to provide some resilience to the Congress.

Mawlong had joined HSPDP, the oldest regional political outfit five years after it was recognised by the Election Commission in 1978. He was pulled towards the party which saw the state as 'an abode of tribals who are a minority, having a separate identity, different and more backward than the other communities'. He shared with the party leaders the desire to preserve, protect and maintain the indigenous rights and identity of the tribals. Mawlong contested from the party as its Umroi candidate, and was elected in the two successive elections after that, in 1988 and 1993, from HSPDP.

At the HSPDP meeting on 20 August 1996, in which he was elected President, EK Mawlong

read out a letter written by Prof GG Swell, elected as Member of Parliament from the Shillong seat in the 1996 Lok Sabha general election, addressed to the former President of the HSPDP, Hopingstone Lyngdoh. In the letter, Prof Swell professed that his election was made possible because of the efforts of the Meghalaya Federation, that jointly supported him in the Lok Sabha election, and exhorted leaders of the HSPDP (Hopingstone Lyngdoh, Evansius Kek Mawlong, Y Fuller Lyngdoh, Tuberlin Lyngdoh) and others to heed the call of the Hill People's Union (HPU) to merge with the Public Demands Implementation Convention (PDIC), HPU, and HSPDP, the state's three major regional parties into one political party. Prof Swell concluded the letter by saying that he firmly stood by the affirmation that unity was the need of the hour in order to fulfil the aspirations of the people.

When the INC formed the Government in the state in 1993, the regional parties strongly felt the need to unite as one because it became a question of survival and relevance. However, as previously mentioned, the lack of discipline owing to frequent defections of legislators often poured cold water on such efforts. The frequent splits and scattered existence of regional political parties made them succumb easily to defections and wore an almost ordinary presence in the state. Added to it was the lack of unity and ideological consistency. Those who split from the HSPDP after the 1993 election

opined that differences arose among the leaders on the question of granting permission for scientific mining of uranium in the state. Some were for it but many were against the contentious issue.

Since 1968, the seeds of dissent were sowed when the HSPDP split from the APHLC. Later, the PDIC and HPU too broke away from the APHLC. The defections of leaders to join the Congress was also frequent and Mawlong had his own interpretation of it. On his election as the new President of the HSPDP, he spoke about reasons why the regional parties such as the HSPDP failed to grow: betrayal by elected leaders.

> These so-called leaders get lured by the lust for gold and silver. Their disregard for the people's mandate, their disloyalty to the regional spirit and sentiment, brings about apathy and mistrust among our supporters at the grassroot. The regional parties have failed to grow because of the selfish actions of our leaders. However, we should not be disheartened. I am of the belief that we will get strong and resolute leaders; those who will not be enticed by the expensive honey of Egyptian Pharaohs.

The leaders of the HPU, PDIC and HSPDP met frequently after this meeting and agreed to dissolve their regional fronts to pave way for the United Democratic Party (UDP). However, as they say, in politics, 'intentions count for nothing, it's action that matters.'

Not all in the HSPDP were in favour of its complete dissolution. A faction, led by Hopingstone Lyngdoh and Tuberlin Lyngdoh, did not concede to the popular demand for unification. As mentioned, prior to the formation of the UDP, the three regional political parties had formally converged under one faction, the Meghalaya Federation with Brington Buhai Lyngdoh as Chairman, and EK Mawlong as General Secretary. The forming of the Meghalaya Federation was seen as a trailer of a movie many had been waiting for. Other than opposition from leaders within the HSPDP, senior leaders too made ambiguous statements that dampened the effort towards unification. After the 1996 Lok Sabha election, BB Lyngdoh announced his opposition to the unification of the three indigenous parties of the state. As it was Prof Swell who mooted the idea to unify the three parties in his letter to the HSPDP, Lyngdoh welcomed Prof Swell to form a new political party but wanted it to 'come under the umbrella of the Meghalaya Federation.'

Despite such setbacks, most of the leaders of the three parties held numerous dialogues and meetings to resolve complex ideological issues and adopt a pragmatic approach. In an Executive Council meeting held in May 1997, EK Mawlong as General Secretary of the Meghalaya Federation said that by the end of June, a committee will look into the details of the unification. The Political Affairs Committee, comprising of fifteen members (three from each

party), was led by BB Lyngdoh as Chairman and was formed in a meeting held at his residence during which all party representatives were present. After almost fifteen years of informal talks, the unity movc was finally about to bear fruit. However, when it finally saw the light of day, the opposition by Hopingstone Lyngdoh towards the complete dissolution of the HSPDP, led to a major tussle within the party. Yet, it was not the first time in its history that the HSPDP was against such an initiative.

In 1985, the HPU was formed by combining a group from the APHLC and a split faction of the HSPDP. At that time too, the parent group of the HSPDP led by Hopingstone Lyngdoh was not in favour of any move that would completely dissolve his party. In 1997, Hopingstone proposed that the other two parties should merge with the HSPDP but most were not in favour because the HPU had more MLAs i.e. ten, whereas, HSPDP and PDIC had only four and two, respectively.

From June till September 1997, there were a series of meetings of the Meghalaya Federation and the individual parties to make the unification move a reality. On 9 June, the Political Affairs Committee of the Meghalaya Federation unanimously decided that a new political party will be formed and the three regional parties will be dissolved. It decided that the three parties should first convene a General Council meeting of their parties to make the decision known to their office bearers and supporters.

The same day, the Youth Wings of the HPU and HSPDP met to express joy over the political development. Likewise, the HPU, Mawlai Circle, the District Committee of the HSPDP Jaiñtia Hills, and the Central Executive Committee of PDIC unanimously supported the move. However, the HSPDP West Khasi Hills opposed a complete dissolution of the party while welcoming the Meghalaya Federation as a platform through which the regional parties could work together.

As far as the HSPDP was concerned, the writing on the wall was clear. The two regional stalwarts—Hopingstone Lyngdoh and EK Mawlong—were heading for a collision. Hopingstone Lyngdoh was of the opinion that the other two parties, the HPU and the PDIC, should dissolve themselves and merge with the HSPDP. However, EK Mawlong was resolute in his decision to completely dissolve all three parties. This led to a division within the HSPDP out of which emerged two factions: the one led by EK Mawlong and the other led by Hopingstone Lyngdoh and others mostly from West Khasi Hills District.

A General Council meeting of the HSPDP, in which the party workers from all over the Khasi and Jaiñtia Hills came together, was convened on 4 July 1997. The main agenda was to take decisions pertaining to all the latest developments. It was a tense situation for many of the party men and leaders because the party by then was a divided house. At the meeting arguments and counter arguments were made on the question of dissolution of the party. The side that was in favour of joining the Meghalaya Federation by dissolving the party wanted to have a vote to get a clear picture and know the mind of the foot soldiers of the party. The side that wasn't in favour of dissolving the party, however, did not agree to this proposal. In the end, the party could not come to any unanimous decision. There were loud dissenting voices and most of them clearly announced that the party was heading for a split. A decision could not be taken and it was resolved that another meeting would be held to discuss the matter again, but no specific date was set for such a meeting.

In the meantime, the Central Executive Committee of the Meghalaya Federation met on 31 July 1997. BB Lyngdoh as the Chairman of the Meghalaya Federation convened the meeting which was attended by EK Mawlong, Hopingstone Lyngdoh, Martle Mukhim, Mihsalan Suchiang, Sanbor Swell Lyngdoh, among many others. They decided that all the selected members would sit together to frame a constitution for the new party to be named United Democratic Party (UDP). The committee should also come up with a proposed party flag and a symbol for the new party. Hopingstone Lyngdoh left the meeting halfway and told the media that in the General Council meeting of the HSPDP held on 4 July, two

differing opinions were expressed and that he was 'not against the unification of the three parties.' It was clear that Hopingstone Lyngdoh was not going to be part of the UDP.

The internal politics of the HSPDP came to a head on 3 September 1997 when the Hopingstone Lyngdoh-led faction decided to suspend EK Mawlong as the party President for 'anti-party activities'. Mawlong, who was away in New Delhi at that time, dismissed the decision when he returned and termed the exercise against the rules of the party as enshrined in its constitution. On 8 September, he called a separate General Council meeting in his capacity as President at the MLA Hostel, Shillong, where the attendees, party workers and office bearers from most of the Khasi-Jaiñtia region supported his leadership and the unification move. HB Dan, President of the Jaiñtia Hills District, presided over the meeting. Some party office bearers from West Khasi Hills District who supported the unification of the three parties, attended the meeting and spoke at length about the political situation. They were Baltasa Nonglang, S Pariong, and A Dkhar. Other prominent leaders from other districts included Dr WT Passah, Staining Nongbri, S Shadap, Shanbor Kurbah, JJ Lyngdoh, Edward Kurbah, Ionis Mawlong, and BK Lyngdoh. Most of these leaders who spoke on the occasion reiterated that the HSPDP will never be able to win sufficient

number of seats in the 1998 General Election to be able form a Government on its own. The aim of the UDP was to fulfil the aspirations of the people, which were alleged to have been unfulfilled by the Indian National Congress. In his speech, EK Mawlong exhorted all the supporters to work hard and didn't fail to mention how Hopingstone Lyngdoh was the first to press for the unification of the regional political parties and had given 'two suggestions: one, to dissolve two out of three parties and merge them with the HSPDP, PDIC or HPU; two, to dissolve all three parties and form a new political dispensation.' The General Council meeting castigated the rival camp's decision to suspend its President and re-elected EK Mawlong as President; HB Dan, E Royal Syiem, HP Shabong and Michael Giri as Vice-Presidents; Constantine Lyngdoh as General Secretary, among others. E Royal Syiem was elected as the new President of the West Khasi Hills District.

This re-election was necessitated following the earlier move of the Hopingstone-faction to suspend EK Mawlong, and electing a different team of office bearers in a separate meeting. In a counter-move, the group led by Mawlong decided to rusticate Tuberlin Lyngdoh, former MLA from Pariong constituency who was in the rival camp, and loyalist of Hopingstone Lyngdoh. The meeting concluded with a firm resolution that the party would merge with the UDP and EK Mawlong and

other leaders of the Meghalaya Federation began the search for candidates to contest the 1998 election under the banner of the new party. They even tried to convince legislators from the Congress, and others who had deserted the regional parties earlier.

H Donkupar Roy Lyngdoh, who won his first election in 1988 on an HSPDP ticket, but later joined the Congress says that he remembers when EK Mawlong won the 1972 elections because his mother, Sentina Lyngdoh was Mawlong's ardent supporter. Their association was strong since the beginning. In 1988, the people of Sohïong constituency had urged him to contest the election and Mawlong too encouraged him 'tremendously.' They had been ministers in the MUPP Government but he joined Congress in 1993 'due to various push and pulls of politics'. During the formation of the UDP, EK Mawlong along with party leaders, Simon Siangshai and SD Khongwir, persuaded him to join the new political party.

> I remember what Bah Mawlong told me that day in his signature calm and composed style. He said, 'Bah Don, please do not have any acrimony towards any of us, and towards me in particular, when you lose the next election.' I confidently replied, 'I will not lose, I will never lose.'

Since HDR Lyngdoh had refused, they put up Rain Augustine Lyngdoh as the UDP candidate in 1998. HDR says that he is glad he 'didn't have any acrimony' towards EK Mawlong even after losing that election.

Mawlong had also approached John A Lyngdoh, another Congressman from Nongspung constituency. Lyngdoh had heard about EK Mawlong as a student of St Dominic's School and knew he was known to help others in need.

> My first meeting with him though was much later when, coincidentally, one truck carrying potatoes from Lyngkhoi village was caught by the police. When I reached the spot near Anjalee Petrol Pump in Shillong, I noticed how Bah Mawlong was already there using his negotiating skills to successfully convince the police to let the truck go.

They met in 1989, when Lyngdoh was elected to the District Council as MDC of the Congress Party. EK Mawlong's oratory skills and statesmanship were on show when he 'tore a Government notification inside the chamber of the Council as it was brought out on a Sunday.' It was seen as a sign of disrespect to the Christian-majority of the state. EK Mawlong visited Lyngdoh after his second election from the Congress to the District Council in 1994, at his residence and requested him to consider joining the new regional party. Mawlong assured him that he will make him an MLA, if he was to consider the request to join the UDP. Lyngdoh says that he was 'touched by his humility because he was already

a prominent figure of the state, a former Minister and Speaker of the Legislative Assembly.' Lyngdoh spoke to the Congress leaders openly about his intention to join the UDP, and formally resigned on 9 September 1997.

> After the formal inauguration of the party, and his election as President, he once called me to his residence and said, 'For you and Bah RA Lyngdoh, I will work tirelessly to ensure that both of you will win together.' And true to his word, he campaigned hard for both our victories in the 1998 election.

The UDP was formally launched on 11 September 1997 during the Joint General Council meeting of the three regional parties after more than five months of concerted efforts. EK Mawlong deliberately chose the day as it coincided with the birthday of his eldest son, George. Martle Mukhim presided over the meeting as Chairman and reports from the individual parties were read out. The reports spelled out the various stages of the unification move and the feedback that was received by the parties from their supporters. This was followed by the formal election of office bearers in which EK Mawlong was elected as President of the new party. Martle Mukhim, AH Scott Lyngdoh, HB Dan and BG Momin were elected as Vice-Presidents, and HAD Sawian, retired IAS officer, as General Secretary, among others.

In his first presidential address to all the

members of the party, EK Mawlong expressed his gratitude to the attendees and spoke about the need to first and foremost serve the interest of the people.

> The many years of effort and struggle has come to life today. Today marks a new beginning in Meghalaya's politics and this party is that beacon of hope for the future of governance in the state...There is a need to undo all the policies of the Congress-led Government that are detrimental for the state. I would like to categorically mention here that all of us should keep the interest of the people first; the party is secondary.

The party was subsequently awarded the Drum or *Ka Nakra* as the party symbol by the Election Commission on 18 December 1997.

Since EK Mawlong had in-depth knowledge and understanding of the problems facing the state, he was instrumental in framing its constitution that encompassed issues like progress of the tribal people while safeguarding their identity, territorial integrity of the state, transparency in governance, safeguarding the environment, and promotion of universal education.

A UNIQUE SPEAKER

THE UDP contested the 1998 general election under EK Mawlong's leadership and won twenty out of the fifty-six seats it contested. Although no other regional party could muster so many numbers ever since the magic of the APHLC in the 1970s, the election resulted in a split mandate, again. The APHLC had won thirty-two seats in the 1972 election but its tally went down to sixteen in 1978. Thus the UDP had done considerably well as other regional parties hardly crossed fifteen seats in any of the preceding elections.

The Congress, which won twenty-five seats after the 1998 election, emerged as the single largest party and was invited by the Governor MM Jacob on 27 February 1998 to form the Government. Salseng C Marak was sworn in as Chief Minister along with DD Lapang, who made a comeback with a thumping win after the 1993 loss as his Deputy. Another prominent personality who was inducted as Minister was Lotsing A Sangma of the Congress. The Government was given time to prove its majority in the forthcoming session. There were objections from other parties, particularly the UDP, that claimed that the Governor had acted in haste by inviting the Congress. EK Mawlong as President of the UDP with vigorous support of the MLAs, was trying his best to negotiate with the other smaller parties including the BJP, HSPDP, People's Democratic Movement (PDM), and some independent MLAs. On the same evening after the Salseng Marak-led Government was sworn in, the elected members of the UDP met at BB Lyngdoh's residence to elect their Parliamentary Party leader. Mawlong proposed the name of their seniormost legislator, BB Lyngdoh, and the decision was supported by AH Scott Lyngdoh and HB Dan, and upheld by other MLAs. Their singular aim was to prevent the Congress from influencing the other MLAs to desert the party.

More than a week later, the Congress was hoping to muster a simple majority of thirty-one legislators to win the post of the Speaker of the House. However, during the Special Session, convened on 10 March, the Congress could not prove its majority in the House. There were only two candidates who filed their nominations for the post of Speaker: Sujit Sangma of the Congress and EK Mawlong from the UDP. When the Pro-

tem Speaker[53] called the House to order on the fateful day, the elected legislators were asked to vote by secret ballot after which Mawlong emerged victorious defeating the Congress nominee by a single vote. It was to be his second and last stint as Speaker.

Since the Government could not muster majority, it lasted only for 12 days, which was the shortest tenure of any Government in the state. The same evening, Salseng C Marak resigned as Chief Minister, paving the way for BB Lyngdoh to form a new Government named the United Parliamentary Forum (UPF), a conglomeration of the UDP, HSPDP, BJP, PDM, the Garo Nationalist Council (GNC) and Independents. BB Lyngdoh was sworn in as Chief Minister that evening, and the next day, his cabinet was expanded with the induction of more ministers.

The Congress, as would any opposition with a large number of MLAs, pulled out all stops to topple the UPF Government. For instance, in June 1998, Maysalin War, the Mawthengkut Legislator resigned as a Minister from her parent party, the HSPDP, and aligned herself with the Opposition. In a letter to the Speaker, War wrote that the HSPDP had spilt due to 'fundamental differences in the implementation of various programmes

53 Pro-tem Speaker is a temporary Speaker appointed for a limited period of time to conduct sessions after elections.'

meant for the interest of the people and the State.' She informed him:

> A new group as the Hill State People Democratic Party (M) has been formed with the undersigned as the Leader. The strength of the new Legislature party is one-third of the HSPDP, in accordance with paragraph 3 of the Tenth Schedule of the Constitution of India.

Hopingstone Lyngdoh filed a complaint to the Speaker requesting him to disqualify Maysalin War as the original party at the grassroot had not split, and she was the only member who decided to leave the party, thus was liable for disqualification under the Tenth Schedule of the Constitution of India.

The matter was informed to the House by Mawlong on 25 June.

Before giving his ruling, Mawlong confessed that he had had a sleepless night, as letters poured in from different representatives till 11:30 pm. He said that since there is enough evidence for prosecuting M War under para 2 of the Tenth Schedule, he was suspending the member and her voting right until a final order was passed by him.

> Today I have received a petition from Srimati M War, where she has only mentioned a split in the legislature party, nothing was mentioned of any split in the original party nor any resolution was adopted in any of the meetings of supporters as she said all active members,

primary members or office bearers have been with her till yesterday.

He also encouraged the House to stop the practice of defection from one group to another group. 'Time has come for us to act as responsible leaders,' he added.

Much to the delight of the Opposition, the UPF Government lasted only for 139 days. On 27 July 1998, the headlines in the media announced that BB Lyngdoh 'had triggered the collapse of his own Government'.[54] In a turn of events that surprised the public, the media and particularly the grassroot workers[55] of the UDP, BB Lyngdoh kicked out all the other parties and joined hands with the Congress. Even some ministers in the Government were taken by surprise. On 27 July, a new Government, named Meghalaya Parliamentary Forum (MPF) was installed with 'Mr Split' BB Lyngdoh as Chief Minister yet again, and DD Lapang as his Deputy.

During the General Meeting of the UDP party workers at Nongpoh, the grassroot leaders questioned the stance of the party and even suggested that it was better for the state to be under President's Rule than work with the Congress. Mawlong, who attended the meeting justified the

54 'Pynkhyllem hi u Bah Bring ïa ka Sorkar UPF.' U Nongsaiñ Hima. 28 July 1998

55 'Lynga ki paidbah ïa ka sorkar MPF, pynshai u President UDP.' U Nongsaiñ Hima. 7 October 1998

reason for aligning with the Congress as a way to ensure a stable Government.

The Congress had tried to topple the UPF Government by enticing other smaller parties, and seven UDP MLAs were also prepared to split from the party to join the Congress. The UDP decided to join hands with the Congress for the stability and longevity of the party, he had reasoned.

Although stability was the reason that was attributed for aligning with the Congress, events that unfolded thereafter made the political situation more complex, and Mawlong had to again pronounce an important ruling that changed the complexion of politics in the state.

In March 1999, the election of Sonia Gandhi as the President of the Congress party triggered an internal squabble and opposition from its members led by Sharad Pawar, Tariq Anwar and Purno A Sangma. Pawar, a former Chief Minister of Maharashtra was a very senior member of the party. Sangma was a former Lok Sabha Speaker and Anwar was also a senior parliamentarian. The trio, whom the media dubbed *Amar, Akbar, Anthony*[56] denoting the disparate religious backgrounds of the three leaders, went on to form a separate party called the Nationalist Congress Party (NCP) or Rashtravadi Congress in May 1999 over the issue of Sonia Gandhi's 'foreign origin'. As President,

56 Title of the 1977 family film by the same name that featured actors Vinod Khanna, Rishi Kapoor, and Amitabh Bachchan in lead roles.

she was pitted to be the leader of the party, and probable Prime Ministerial candidate in the impending September-October 1999 Lok Sabha elections. Pawar admitted to have been insecure after reports of Sonia Gandhi staking claim to form the Government after the fall of Atal Bihari Bajpayee's dispensation in 1999.[57] He fancied either Dr Manmohan Singh or himself as Prime Minister.

There were reports that formation of the NCP would have its impact on Meghalaya as Sangma was visiting the state, and the rumour was that he wished to split the Congress party by luring sitting MLAs to join his new party.

Purno Sangma, who was a close friend of Mawlong, had called him before breaking away from the Congress. When Mawlong advised him to restrain from doing so, the strongman from Garo Hills simply told him that they'd talk in person two days later over a traditional Khasi dinner at EK Mawlong's house. On 30 May 1999, Mawlong told Sangma that the Congress party had given Sangma more than he could have asked for. Notwithstanding his immense calibre, his elevation to the post of Union Minister and Speaker of the Lok Sabha, wouldn't have been possible without the blessing of the Congress. Hence, breaking away from it would tantamount to restarting his career in

57 https://www.indiatoday.in/india/story/i-quit-congress-after-sonia-gandhi-staked-her-claim-to-pm-s-post-in-1999-sharad-pawar-1174856-2018-02-22

national politics, which Mawlong suggested wasn't going to be easy. Sangma argued that Sonia Gandhi was adamant to lead the party, and splitting from the Congress was the best way to show their dissent and disagreement to the impending rise of a foreign national to the Prime Ministership of the country.

Purno Sangma's visit to Shillong triggered a lot of speculation over the survival of the Meghalaya Government. And indeed there was a twist.

Nine of the twenty-five Congress legislators led by Lotsing A Sangma, split from the Congress to form the Meghalaya Congress Legislature Party (MCLP), who later formally joined the NCP. The other eight were Adolf Lu Hitler R Marak, Admiral K Sangma, Brening A Sangma, Methrona Marak, Beckstar K Sangma, Elston D Marak, Abdus Saleh, and Monindra Rava. All the rebel legislators were from the Garo Hills, and their breaking away from the Congress indicated the enormous respect and influence that Purno A Sangma commanded.

After the split in the Congress party, the impending disqualification of the nine MLAs was a hot potato. As Speaker, Mawlong could either recognise the split as a legal one or disqualify the members from the Assembly for contravening the rules of the Tenth Schedule of the Constitution. So the survival of Purno A Sangma's new dispensation in Meghalaya rested in Mawlong's hands.

On 22 June, Mawlong pronounced his ruling validating the split in the Indian National Congress

pertaining to Meghalaya which took place on 31 May 1999 both at the level of the original political party and at the level of the legislature party. Since the new split group, the 'Meghalaya Congress Legislature Party' commanded the required number of more than one-third of the total strength of twenty-five members of the Congress Legislature Party, it did not merit disqualification under para 3 of the Tenth Schedule of the Constitution. Thus, the nine MLAs survived a looming disqualification. More significantly, the emergence of Purno A Sangma's NCP in Meghalaya wasn't truncated prematurely.

In the aftermath of the September 1999 Lok Sabha election from the Shillong Parliamentary seat, the MPF was in jitters yet again. Patty Ripple Kyndiah of the Congress defeated his nearest rival SD Khongwir of the UDP by a margin of 37,823 votes. In the Tura Parliamentary seat, Purno A Sangma decimated Congress' Atul C Marak by 1,13,579 votes.[58]

The result in Shillong embittered the already disheartened UDP workers in the Khasi-Jaiñtia Hills, who blamed the party's alignment with the Congress for the loss. Eventually, the UDP broke ties with the Congress and roped in the nine legislators of the NCP along with three from the BJP, and PDM on 12 October. EK Mawlong was offered a ministry in the UDP as BB Lyngdoh's

58 http://ceomeghalaya.nic.in/election-history/general-election-to-lok-sabha/1999-ls.pdf

Deputy, but he declined for the second time. In the UDP-Congress Government, BB Lyngdoh had offered the same post to him, but he refused saying a small state like Meghalaya didn't require two Deputy Chief Ministers, as DD Lapang was already in the ministry as the Deputy Chief Minister.

Apart from conducting the proceedings in a fair manner, EK Mawlong, in his two stints as Speaker contributed to the cause of the Legislative Assembly in other ways. Terence Cajee, former Secretary of the House in an article[59] published to commemorate the Silver Jubilee of the Assembly wrote that the Third House (1983-88) presided over by Mawlong was the most eventful insofar as the Assembly Secretariat was concerned. He ensured that the Chamber of the House was modified and furnished to suit the new Meghalaya Legislature. The Chamber was used right from the time of undivided Assam. He also proposed to build a new Members' Hostel and an independent press under the Assembly Secretariat. An important official event in 1986, the SAARC Conference, was also held in the Assembly premises with Prime Minister Rajiv Gandhi in attendance. In 1987, the joint celebration of the Golden Jubilee of the composite Assam Legislature and the sitting of the Committee of Presiding Officers presided by the

59 The Meghalaya Legislative Assembly Since its Inception–Some Reminisces. Silver Jubilee Celebration Souvenir (1972-1997). pp. 65-67

Deputy Speaker, Lok Sabha was held.

In his first stint as Speaker of the Meghalaya Legislative Assembly, EK Mawlong met the then Deputy Chairman of the Planning Commission, Dr Manmohan Singh and sought financial assistance for setting up the Meghalaya Legislative Assembly printing press. The former Prime Minister gracefully accepted and the press stands till date, printing numerous documents required by the Assembly and other Government agencies.

His first stint as Speaker, though, was a rather unique one. As a Speaker and Legislator, Mawlong shared a good rapport with leaders across all party lines, one of who was Captain Williamson A Sangma. After the 1983 election, BB Lyngdoh of the APHLC, who had shared power with Congress' Capt Sangma in the previous term, chose to align with the HSPDP, PDIC and Independent legislators to form the Meghalaya United Parliamentary Party (MUPP) ministry. However, the fault lines in the Government were clearly visible beginning with the election of the Speaker. EK Mawlong, the candidate put up by the BB Lyngdoh group, was elected to become the youngest Speaker of the House at the age of 37, but he secured three votes less than expected. In the election of the Deputy Speaker, another surprise sprung up when the APHLC's Mackenson Sangma lost to Ira Marak of the Congress. On 31 March 1983, the 25-day-old MUPP ministry, was voted out owing

to the defection of legislators, including four from HSPDP, one from the PDIC and one independent. This paved the way for Capt Williamson A Sangma to take over as Chief Minister once again.[60] A disappointed BB Lyngdoh commented ruefully, 'People let us down because of personal grievances. You cannot satisfy everybody.'[61] Perhaps Lyngdoh was alluding to the difficulty in accommodating MLAs who aspired for ministerial berths or those who hankered for better portfolios.

It was a precarious situation for Mawlong as he could have been removed at any time. This was because he was also a member of the HSPDP, which was pushed to the Opposition. However, he remained in the chair till the end of the term because of his closeness to Capt Sangma. In an obituary to his leader and friend, Mawlong spoke about working with Sangma as a Speaker from 1983 to 1987:

> Captain Sangma, as some of the Hon'ble Members have reminded, was a great democrat. When I attended the Presiding Officers' Conference [in Srinagar] when we discussed with other Presiding Officers of other Legislatures, they were surprised when I said that I belonged to the Opposition. They said that it is

60 https://www.indiatoday.in/magazine/indiascope/story/19830430-captain-williamson-sangma-to-lead-coalition-government-in-meghalaya-771355-2013-10-19

61 ibid

> very unique in this country to have a Speaker from the Opposition at that time. I told them that we have got a good understanding in the House and I think it is due to Captain Sangma and some of our colleagues who were working with him at that time. Therefore, in my life, I found that he is one of the great leaders for whom I have a lot of respect. Captain Sangma has left behind a long history. It is for us to emulate his footprints and good examples.

His two eventful stints as Speaker of the Assembly were also years of political turmoil, and as an impartial player, he had to deal with challenging upheavals. EL Lyttan, former Secretary of the Legislative Assembly, spoke about Mawlong's understanding of administrative matters as 'exemplary.' He also praised the orders he passed and notings in files for his efficiency. He wrote:[62]

> In his two terms as Speaker, I had the opportunity to know him better, closer and also the privilege to understand his mind, his wisdom, his knowledge and his ability. He was not only adept with the rules, but also an able administrator. His 'Rulings' and 'Directions' which he gave in the House from time to time, and the spirit of impartiality which he showed to all members of the House illustrated his

62 Obituary on EK Mawlong by EL Lyttan

> sincerity to uphold the dignity of this high and dignified office... It was an honour to serve under him, the choice to elect him as Speaker twice was really worthy and wise.'

His second term as Speaker was cut short on 8 March 2000 after about two years in the dignified chair as the state, which had already witnessed four different governments since 1998, was gearing up for yet another political cyclone. And, Mawlong was about to be strapped to the cyclone's eyewall.

SEVENTH CHIEF MINISTER

DURING A meeting of the Legislature Party of the United Democratic Party, the sitting Chief Minister, BB Lyngdoh, decided to resign from the post owing to advanced age.[63] A demand for change in leadership was put forward by PT Sawkmie, a UDP Legislator and Minister in the Lyngdoh cabinet, who was at the forefront of the demand, was quoted saying that there was restlessness amongst a section of UDP Ministers and MLAs. They wanted a change of leadership in the Government not just because of Lyngdoh's health concerns but also because they felt 'there were certain outside forces dictating terms.' Displeased with the way the show was being run, the UDP ministers approached EK Mawlong two or three times in his official Speaker's chamber

63 'Mawlong wrests mantle from Lyngdoh.' The Meghalaya Guardian. March 7, 2000.

in the Legislative Assembly as he was the next senior-most leader, an experienced statesman, and president of the party.

A reluctant Mawlong was of the opinion that any change should not take place forcefully, especially against the wishes of the respectable Lyngdoh. It was only after enough support was rallied from the MLAs and ministers of the coalition, that the ministers could convince Mawlong to 'take over in the interest of the party and efficient governance.'

On 8 March 2000, Evansius Kek Mawlong, at the age of 54, was thus sworn in as the seventh Chief Minister of Meghalaya by the Governor of Meghalaya, MM Jacob, succeeding the veteran BB Lyngdoh. The swearing-in ceremony was held at the Raj Bhawan in Shillong in the presence of many political leaders, officers, relatives, and supporters. Mawlong was decked in Khasi traditional finery; a turban made of fine silk wound around his head.

Having been in public service for more than twenty-five years, Mawlong was well acquainted with the problems of the state. Like any responsible leader, he had noble intentions to usher in accelerated growth particularly in resolving the border dispute with Assam, and improving education and health sectors. However, the time of his succession, in retrospect, was perhaps not conducive for smooth and unhindered governance. The 1990s as well as the first decade of the new millennium were marked by violence of insurgency across the entire state.

Militant organisations, including the Hynñiewtrep Achik Liberation Council (HALC), which later split into the Hynñiewtrep National Liberation Council (HNLC) and the Achik Matgrik Liberation Army (AMLA), and subsequent rise of other insurgent forces like the Achik National Volunteers' Council (ANVC) posed major challenges on the law and order front.[64] The beginning of the 1990s saw frequent bandhs called by militant organisations, shoot-outs, extortions and kidnappings, resulting in the killings of civilians and police personnel even during the second decade of the new millennium. Pressure groups and students' organisations that were active in the Khasi-Jaiñtia Hills since the late 1970s also resorted to office picketing, strikes and violent confrontation with the state machinery to press for various demands, including implementation of the Inner Line Permit Regulation System, amendment in the Job Reservation Policy, creation of 10,000 jobs in the state, among many other demands.

In fact, in his first press meet as the head of the new coalition Government, the Meghalaya Parliamentary Forum, which comprised of the United Democratic Party (UDP), the Nationalist Congress Party (NCP), the Bharatiya Janata Party (BJP), and the People's Democratic Movement (PDM), he appealed to the insurgent groups to

64 'CM shares Opposition concern on law and order.' The Meghalaya Guardian. 4 April 2000

abstain from violence and welcomed them for unconditional talks with the Government. He spoke at length about ensuring development and security, which remained his priorities during his term as the CM. Besides, he emphasised on the need to usher development in other spheres including agriculture, education, industries, road, communication, and employment. For Mawlong, peace and development shared a symbiotic relationship. As the Chief Minister, he held the portfolios of Cabinet Affairs, Political, Law, Personnel and Administrative Reforms.

In his short tenure of eighteen months as Chief Minister, EK Mawlong tried to resolve many pending problems, including the border dispute with the state of Assam and brought in fresh and innovative ideas to usher positive change in the lives of many.

Inter-State Boundary Dispute

Five days after being sworn in as Chief Minister, Mawlong convened a meeting with the state political leaders and officers to discuss the border dispute before taking it up with his Assam counterpart, Prafulla Kumar Mahanta. Thereafter, on 15 March 2000, the two Chief Ministers, along with a host of ministers, MLAs and the three Chief Executive Members of the three District Councils of the State, met at Dispur to discuss the long pending border dispute. The two heads of governments resolved to

conduct a 'field demarcation in those sectors of the border areas where there were no differences. In sectors where there are differences, the contentious issues were to be discussed at the Chief Secretary level within a period of six months. As regards Block I and Block II of Assam's Karbi Anglong District, the two Chief Ministers agreed to make a joint visit to the areas and discuss the related issues to arrive at a decision on the matter.'[65] The two Chief Ministers met again in April 2000 at Dispur after trouble erupted in the Maikhuli area in Block I after which they decided to jointly visit both the disputed blocks that bordered Karbi Anglong.

The joint visit of the two Chief Ministers to the disputed areas of Block I and Block II, on 11 May 2000 was a first in the history of the two states. Thousands of locals gathered to greet the two leaders in the public rally. Those in Block I, who considered themselves to be a part of Jaiñtia Hills urged Mawlong to take necessary steps to re-transfer the areas that the Assam Government claimed under the Karbi Anglong District. In his speech, Mawlong urged the district administration to ensure that those residing in the Blocks were accorded good treatment. Mahanta and Mawlong together assured that they 'will make the best efforts to arrive at an amicable settlement.' Both the Chief Ministers resolved to settle the long pending issue

65 'State Assam to resolve border issue.' *The Meghalaya Guardian,* 16 March 2000

within six months.

When they met again on 21 December, it was decided that the Deputy Commissioners of Jaiñtia Hills and Karbi Anglong districts would conduct a survey, and that the District Councils of both the states would be consulted before finalising the transfer of land. Mawlong proposed that villages, where the Khasi-Jaiñtia were in majority, should be re-transferred to Meghalaya, if they have been included under Assam's jurisdiction. There was also talk of resolving the long-pending issue through a 'give and take manner' which met with objections and mild hostility, particularly from leaders of Karbi Anglong.[66]

The two Chief Ministers, both strong regional leaders of their respective states, got along quite well, and shared mutual respect. The constitution of the Chandrachund Boundary Committee in 1985 by former Chief Ministers Hiteswar Saikia and Captain Williamson A Sangma, headed by the former Chief Justice of India YV Chandrachund, was the first step that exhibited a political will to resolve the boundary dispute amicably though it didn't yield the desired result. The effort by Mawlong and his Assam counterpart exhibited immense sincerity to end the boundary dispute, but unfortunately the Prafulla Mahanta-led Assam Gana Parishad (AGP) Government couldn't retain

66 https://www.telegraphindia.com/india/meghalaya-not-to-take-assam-land/cid/937987

power in the state in the 2001 election, and the INC led by Tarun Gogoi wrested the reign from the regional party. Mawlong could not reignite the magic that he had created with Mahanta perhaps due to ideological differences with the new Congress regime in Assam, and the dispute continues to remain alive till this day.

Decongesting Shillong

One of the major issues that Mawlong frequently raised in the Legislative Assembly as the Opposition member was the issue of growing congestion in Shillong. His efforts to convince the Defence authorities to donate portions of unused land for public use became successful when Major General VK Dua and the Cantonment Board agreed to hand over four plots of land located at Jhalupara near Mahavir Park, and commercial areas at Luckier Road (Garikhana), Butcher Road, and at Ïew Mawlong opposite the popular Anjalee Cinema Hall. In fact, after carrying out an inspection on 1 September, the plot at Luckier Road was used to build a parking lot for a shopping complex, particularly for outstation commercial vehicles of Ri Bhoi District, and the one at Jhalupara became an electric crematorium as the non-tribal population in the city wished to cremate their dead without using firewood.

On 6 November, a Memorandum of Understanding was signed and a public function

organised at Ïew Mawlong, one of the busiest commercial areas, to hand over the documents.

The following year on 1 April 2001, Mawlong laid the foundation stone for the construction of a shopping complex and a parking lot at Luckier Road (Garikhana). The construction of the parking lot was completed in 2005 and it has helped in easing traffic congestion in the Ïewduh area to a large extent.

Taking administration closer to people

Mawlong was a firm believer in actively solving people's problems and hence, made sure to visit district headquarters to monitor and review the progress of developmental schemes. During these visits, he met officials of different departments to learn about the problems faced in implementing the various initiatives. When he visited Tura, one of the largest towns in the state in July, he was informed that the long pending plan for development and beautification of Tura town had already been prepared and that the tender for the work would be floated. On noticing that the State Government wasn't able to provide 25 per cent funding to implement the scheme prepared by the District Rural Development Authority, he requested the then Prime Minister, Atal Bihari Vajpayee to revise the center-state share from 75:25 to 90:10. The beautification of the town was later taken up by successive governments.

During the Budget Session of the year 2000, he reiterated the need to take the administration closer to people. In 1970, the state had only two districts, United Khasi-Jaiñtia Hills, and Garo Hills. Later, seven districts, eight civil sub-divisions, many administrative units and block headquarters were created to bring the administration closer to the people.

> Now there is proposal also to create seven more Blocks with the sole intention to bring administration to the people. We are also exercising our mind, that in order to make BDOs (Block Development Officer) more effective we are also trying to give them more power. In that way the people needn't come to the capital (and) they will meet only the BDO (and) people will be able to solve the problems.

On 24 March 2001, the first of the seven new Block Development Offices were inaugurated at Jirang in Ri Bhoi District. At the inaugural function, Mawlong said that about 71 villages with a population of about 20,000 will gain from this newly established Block Office. Even though Umroi needed a separate Block Office and it was one of the popular demands of the people, Mawlong gave preference to Jirang as he felt that the people of Jirang faced more inconveniences while travelling to the Block Office in Umsning as the distance was farther, and the condition of the roads was more

pathetic. He felt that Umroi could wait for its turn in the subsequent years as road communication between Umroi and Umsning wasn't that difficult as compared to Jirang.

On 6 April 2001, he inaugurated the second new Community and Rural Development Block Office at Saipung in Jaintia Hills District which would serve the need of more than 25,000 people living in more than 70 villages. A fortnight later along with former CM BB Lyngdoh, he inaugurated the Khat-Ar Shnong Community and Rural Development Block. He urged the people to avail the opportunities and benefits made available to them by the Government.

Dealing with Insurgency

The late 1990s and early 2000s were beset with militant activities not only in Meghalaya but in the entire North-East. As Chief Minister, he exhorted the Chief Ministers of all the insurgency-infested North-Eastern states to work together to bring peace. In one of the meetings with the Assam Chief Minister, Prafulla Kumar Mahanta, Mawlong suggested him to take the lead, being the head of Government of the biggest North-Eastern State, in convening a common meeting of all the Chief Ministers of the sister states.

On 12 May, a North-East Chief Ministers' Conference was held in Shillong and a resolution taken to jointly eliminate insurgency from the

North-East. The Chief Ministers decided to meet and discuss with the Central Government and apprise it of the innumerable problems that arose due to the militancy and insurgency. They also resolved to meet the Prime Minister to help strengthen the financial condition of the states. In his address at the Chief Ministers' Conference, Mawlong reminded the Chief Ministers the pressing needs facing the region like unresolved inter-state boundary disputes, the need to constitute a North-East Chief Ministers' Forum to check unabated influx of foreign nationals, and the need to organise a Peace Rally in the entire North-East as an attempt to exhort the militants to end violence and return to mainstream.

Soon a Peace Rally was organised in all the state capitals, district headquarters, and civil sub-divisions of all the North-Eastern states urging all militant organisations to shun violence and resolve their grievances through dialogue with the Government. In Shillong, thousands of people from all walks of life including students, parents, common folk, public representatives, bureaucrats and police personnel attended the rally at the Jawaharlal Nehru Stadium. A procession began from Fire Brigade Ground, Laitumkhrah and culminated in the stadium, where school and college students had already gathered with slogans. Prayers, invocations, and devotional songs presented by people across all faiths were offered on

the singular theme, 'Give Peace a Chance'. Though the Peace Rally was a noble initiative in sensitising the people about the grave challenges posed by militancy, the violence and bloodshed continued unabated.

Mawlong would forcefully declare that peace and tranquility were important for the smooth implementation of development programmes. In March 2000, he signed an agreement with Prafulla Kumar Mahanta for cooperation among the two states of Assam and Meghalaya in countering insurgency. He appealed to everyone in the state, including the Opposition in the Assembly to extend their cooperation to the Government to tackle the problem of insurgency He welcomed the ban imposed by the Government of India that outlawed the ANVC and HNLC on 26 November 2000. Although the Government was fighting quite earnestly to end militant activities, it did not extend support to the Prevention of Terrorism Activities (POTA) Bill on the ground that law and order and insurgency in the State did not warrant having such legislation. The POTA Bill which ultimately became an Act was one of the most controversial anti-terrorism legislations in India. After its passage there were allegations of the Act being used for political vendetta. More than 250 people including South Indian politician, Vaiko[67] were arrested

67 'SP condemns Vaiko's arrest under Pota' The Times of India, 13 July 2002.

under the Act. The Mawlong Government too felt that the law could be taken advantage of by the law enforcement agencies. The Act was ultimately repealed by the Indian Parliament in 2004.

Mawlong was able to bring the ANVC, which was a militant group based in the Garo Hills, to negotiate a peace treaty with the Government. However, several attempts to reach out to the HNLC, a group that spread terror in the Khasi and Jaiñtia Hills, failed despite the fact that two prominent church leaders, Archbishop Dominic Jala and Bishop Purely Lyngdoh from the Khasi-Jaiñtia Church Leaders Forum were part of the talks.

Despite efforts by all stakeholders, the actions of the militant groups turned even more ghastly when on 5 January 2001, five people were shot dead in broad daylight in the heart of Shillong.[68] A few masked men stepped out of a vehicle carting AK-56 and AK-47 rifles and sprayed bullets indiscriminately through the tall glass windows of a shop in Dhanketi. The dead included three shopkeepers and two young men from nearby Malki locality. On 16 May, an attempt to loot a bank at Lumdiengjri was foiled by the police but the security guard of the bank, Lal Thabah, was shot dead.[69] There were several other cases of killings and extortions.

68 *'Ther kuli ha dukan TV, ïap 5 ngut, mynsaw 4.'* U Nongsaiñ Hima. 6 January 2001.

69 *'Siat ïap 4 kuli ïa u nongap pahara.'* U Nongsaiñ Hima. 17 May 2001.

Better Healthcare

Mawlong played a key role in ensuring the commencement of the construction of the North-East Indira Gandhi Regional Institute of Health and Medical Sciences (NEIGRIHMS). The hospital located at Mawdiangdiang in the outskirts of Shillong, which now caters to patients from almost all over the North-East and also offers MBBS and nursing courses, was conceptualised in 1987. The work relating to the setting up of its permanent campus began when Mawlong was at the helm and the foundation stone was laid by Dr CP Thakur, the Union Health Minister on 8 August 2000. Dr Thakur gave a detailed description of the plan for the hospital and Mawlong in turn thanked the Minister for his efforts in finally fulfilling the 'long awaited dream which lasted for one and a half decades.' He urged Dr Thakur to consider increasing the number of MBBS and BDS seats in the interest of the candidates of Meghalaya, and stressed on the need to give first preference to qualified local candidates for non-technical posts.

Mawlong also put great emphasis on the improvement of infrastructure in the state health department and he travelled to the district headquarters to know the ground realities. When he visited Tura, he was shocked at the manner in which the patients were being treated at the Tura Tuberculosis Hospital. The inadequate infrastructure in the Garo Hills prompted him

to urge the Health Department to prepare a comprehensive plan to improve the health facilities. On 14 April 2000, during a felicitation programme held at Nongpoh, Mawlong proclaimed that the Ri Bhoi District, blessed by nature, should be developed in all spheres including healthcare. He promised to upgrade the existing Primary Community Health and on 4 June the same year, which was the anniversary of the Ri Bhoi District Foundation Day, Mawlong inaugurated the upgraded centre which had 100 beds and better facilities to cater to the growing population.

A month before, he had already laid the foundation stone for two upgraded Primary Health Centres at Mawlong village. At the inauguration, a concerned Mawlong promised to improve the capacity of the Shillong Civil Hospital from 400 to 600 beds to accommodate more in-patients, and also to make provisions for an ICU as the hospital did not have a separate ICU then.

Special Focus on Education

In his first Budget Session as the Chief Minister, Mawlong expressed concern about the lack of a dignified treatment meted out to teachers. When Opposition members raised concerns about the irregularity of payment of salary of teachers in the grant-in-aid schools, he assured them that steps had been taken to disburse the salary every month. Aggrieved teachers had marched the streets in

protest against the delay and non-payment of their dues for several months. Replying to a discussion on the issue on 3 April 2000, Mawlong stated:

> The Finance Minister has ensured to disburse timely the salary to educational institutions by streamlining the present system…we will make all efforts to see that all teachers get their salaries in time.

In order to fulfill the various demands of teachers and to improve education, he proposed to cut down on avoidable expenditure in order to judiciously use the limited resources of the State. Depending upon the financial position of the state, he vowed to provide facilities, especially to those villages where there were no schools, or single-teacher schools to provide them with more teachers.

During his visit to the headquarter of West Garo Hills in Tura, Mawlong informed that the financial assistance received from the World Bank would be utilised to establish a Polytechnic in the town and another at Jowai. At that time, there was only one Polytechnic located in Shillong. He believed that the need of the hour was to produce employable young men and women, and polytechnics would help solve the unemployment problem in the state. The first academic session of the Tura Polytechnic started in 2001 and the one in Jowai in 2002.

The Government also undertook a rapid upgradation of schools in rural areas, and took steps

to set up Inspectorate of schools in all the District Headquarters to improve the quality of education. The Government also facilitated the completion of the Jaiñtia Eastern College at Khliehriat, an institution which was erected largely due to the generous contribution of the people of the area. On the request of Dr Ananya Guha, Former Regional Director of the Indira Gandhi National Open University (IGNOU) to help the Regional Centre find a permanent place for their campus in Shillong, Mawlong helped in getting approval for the allotment of a plot of land within the NEHU Permanent Campus at Mawkynroh, Shillong. The centre had been operating from a temporary building located at Nongthymmai since 1988.

There were other initiatives taken by him as Chief Minister in the power sector which included restarting the disbanded Sonapani Mini Hydel Heritage Project in Shillong, and the Myntdu Leshka Hydro Electric Project at Jaiñtia Hills. A proposal to create a budget provision for the Chief Minister's Special Urban and Rural Development Fund amounting to Rs 1 crore and Rs 4 crore for the urban and rural constituencies, respectively, was passed in the Assembly during his tenure. The expansion of the Umroi Airport by another thirty-seven acres at a cost of Rs 35 crore was also initiated in June 2000. The creation of a corpus fund for the welfare of journalists was also initiated, but nothing was done thereafter by successive governments and

it remains an unfulfilled aspiration.

As Chief Minister, he deliberated in regional and national level meetings, and highlighted the issue of regional disparity in the field of development between the North-Eastern States and other parts of India and reiterated the importance of bridging that gap.

Pressure Groups' Agitations

On 6 August 2001 at about nine at night, unidentified miscreants hurled stones at Mawlong's private residence at Lumsohphoh, Lower Mawprem. At that time, the entire family had temporarily vacated the residence and was staying at the Tara Ghar Bungalow near Ward's Lake, which was the official residence of the Chief Minister. His private house was looked after by a relative who was staying with her three children. When the sound of the shattering glasses alerted the tenants who were staying a floor below the main house, one of the tenants ran out to ascertain what was happening. On seeing the worried man, one of the stone throwers whose face was concealed, shouted at the tenant by name and told him to return. Though there were Home Guards deputed to protect the house, they were helpless as the attackers were standing on higher ground. So the guards too ran for cover. By the time the police arrived, a lot of damage had already been done to the house, but fortunately none were hurt.

The incident occurred at the peak of the agitation spearheaded by the Khasi Students' Union (KSU). The union was formed in 1978 to protect the interests of the Khasi community particularly against non-indigenous communities whom they perceived as usurpers of the rights and interests of the indigenous tribals. Uncharacteristically, under its President, Paul Lyngdoh, the KSU accelerated its agitation during Mawlong's tenure. It was a never-before-seen aggression to compel the Government to meet its demands, which were in reality politically unviable. The intensive agitations began in May 2001, when the KSU submitted a charter of demands to the Government which included the amendment of the Job Reservation Policy of the state, implementation of the Inner Line Regulation, acceptance of 1951 as cut-off year for identifying the indigenous population, amending the Land Transfer Act to prevent other tribal communities from purchasing land in the state, relocating the Education Board to the capital city as it was located in Tura, creation of 10,000 jobs in the state, and handing over of cases involving corruption to the CBI. Most of these demands were not new and were being made right from the 1980s. The Union re-ignited them through a series of agitations to pressurise the Government to fulfill all of them and initiated a protest called the *Ksan Rngiew* Movement in September 2000.[70]

70 Srikanth, H. *Prospects of Liberal Democracy in Meghalaya*. Economic and Political Weekly. Vol. 40, Issue No. 36, 03 Sep, 2005

The most vigorous agitation was for amendment of the Job Reservation Policy. The policy which was implemented in 1972, has a fixed quota of 40 per cent for the Khasi-Jaiñtia community, 40 per cent for the Garos, and 20 per cent for other tribes and general category. The KSU demanded a restructuring of the reservation policy with 50:30:20 per cent. To pressurise the Government, the KSU called bandhs, did office picketing, and even staged a hunger strike calling for Mawlong's resignation for failing to fulfill the demands. Bindo M Lanong, as Chief Organiser of the UDP denigrated the demands for Mawlong's resignation owing to the agitations that had disturbed normal life, and reminded the agitators that the various demands made by the KSU were inherited by the Government from other governments of the past right from 1972, and all such inherited issues cannot be solved overnight by any Government.[71] Mawlong's supporters and detractors alike though, felt he was too soft towards the pressure groups, and that his leniency was used as a leverage to create further pandemonium in the state. Commentators thought that he should have given the police a freer hand in stringently dealing with those instigators who raised unrealistic demands simply to project and propel themselves before the public as the next generation political leaders of the state.

71 ' Lanong defends Mawlong.' The Meghalaya Guardian. August 30, 2001.

The Government tried to placate the agitators by agreeing to look into most of the demands and constituting various committees to study their feasibility, but it was met with stiff opposition particularly from the Government's ally, the Nationalist Congress Party (NCP) and the Garo Students' Union.[72]

The unprecedented protests culminated prior to the fall of the Government without any resolution. The demands were never reignited with the same vitriolic fervor and hostility. The KSU President, Paul Lyngdoh, like his predecessor Bull N Lyngdoh, contested the general election to the Legislative Assembly in 2003, and was elected from Jaïaw constituency. Despite winning three times from the constituency, and rule of seven different governments since 2003, he couldn't get the governments to bring in the changes he so ardently fought for on the streets of Shillong.

In a letter to Roshan Warjri, a cabinet colleague, Mawlong expressed dismay for not being able to work freely in a tranquil atmosphere as he had to deal with multifarious elements like the underground militants and the over-ground agitators. He expressed that their actions were 'inimical to his efforts in bringing peace, progress and development' and the animosity had turned personal, as even his private residence was not spared.

72 'Furore in Garo Hills over move to review quota', *The Meghalaya Guardian,* 14 September 2001

While deliberating about such activities on most occasions he dismissed the pressure tactics of the KSU and raised concerns why a student organisation wanted to meddle in matters that were untenable. He believed that the over-zealous leaders, who gave long lectures on the streets, felt it was very easy to make overnight changes to policies that were framed since the inception of the state. However, legislative procedures take time and the tactics to pressurise the Government by calling bandhs for weeks was simply a waste of resources and affected livelihood, especially for the daily wage earners. Though the state had witnessed massive deterioration of law and order in 1978, 1987, and 1992 owing to communal riots, the KSU agitation was perhaps the first-of-its-kind political demonstration that curtailed the normal functioning of the Government but was bereft of any productive outcome.

Though his tenure as Chief Minister was a short one that was rife with law and order issues, PR Hing, his Private Secretary for two years, remembers Mawlong as a kind and helpful leader, one who always invited him to have food with him. In 2001, when they were returning from an interview with Aaj Tak in New Delhi, Mawlong told Hing how for long Meghalaya and its people had been isolated and that he would try his 'best to project the image of the state in a better way'. Hing added that Mawlong 'could be regionalistic as well as nationalistic, blending the two sensibilities together beautifully.'

TROUBLE OVER A HOUSE

IN 1991, EK Mawlong, then a Minister of the General Administration Department (GAD) in the BB Lyngdoh ministry, met Jyoti Basu, incumbent Chief Minister of West Bengal, to provide a plot of land in Kolkata to construct a new Meghalaya House. Although there was already one at Russell Street, the state's Public Works Department recommended that the building be reconstructed owing to its age. In the interim, it would be a great inconvenience for travelers if they didn't have a place to halt, Mawlong argued. The Government of West Bengal provided land at Kasba.

The Government since 1984 had also considered building a commercial complex within Meghalaya House at Russell Street in order to generate revenue, but the plan was never taken forward. However, the idea for reconstruction of Meghalaya House at Russell Street later mooted in 1999 during the tenure of BB Lyngdoh as Chief

Minister. The matter was discussed at a cabinet meeting in February 2000, and the Government instructed the General Administration Department (GAD) to explore ways and means to obtain funds for the purpose.[73]

With the swearing-in of Mawlong as Chief Minister on 8 March 2000, he inherited the matter.

A fortnight after the swearing-in, the matter relating to reconstruction of Meghalaya House was discussed in the State Assembly during its Budget Session. Nimarson Momin, the GAD Minister in Mawlong's ministry, informed that an office-cum-commercial complex was to be built chiefly for generation of revenue, but the project could not materialise due to indecision on the part of successive governments since 1984-85. Nimarson Momin said that the complex will be built on a joint venture basis as the Government was 'not in a position to provide' Rs 15 crore. According to the minister, the State Government will have a share of freehold 79 cottahs (*kattha*) which cannot be sold or transferred. The firm which undertakes the entire construction shall be providing the financial share.

On 20 July, a Notice Inviting Tender (NIT) was floated for a joint venture project with the Government of Meghalaya to construct the office-cum-commercial complex at 9/10 Russell Street, Kolkata.

73 'Mawlong: Nothing wrong with Kolkata Land Deal', *The Shillong Times, 22 February 2002*

The cabinet decided that 'detailed guidelines on the terms and conditions for the offer' would be prepared. While the State Government had sought the opinion of the Departments of Law, Revenue, Public Works and Finance on the preparation of the draft bid, there was delay in receiving the views, and hence, the opening of tenders was extended. On 2 November, the cabinet withdrew the tender as it felt that the terms and conditions of the NIT were inadequate.

The tender was finally opened in mid-February after a committee constituted by the GAD under the orders of the cabinet, examined the proposal for reconstruction and setting up of the complex. The committee was led by the Chief Secretary, JP Singh, and had senior officers from Departments of Finance, Planning, Public Works, Urban Affairs, Revenue, Law and General Administration.

In August-September, the Chief Secretary placed the file before Mawlong, the Chief Minister, for his approval to extend the time for calling the tender on the ground that more time was required to study the terms and conditions of the draft tender, which were not found satisfactory. Although he approved the extension, the Chief Secretary, JP Singh, asked for the constitution of a High Power Committee comprising officers from key departments of the Government, to examine the matter. The State Cabinet constituted the High Powered Committee chaired by the Chief Secretary,

and after obtaining the views of the Department of Finance, GAD, PWD and Revenue, the committee ultimately approved the idea of setting up the project on a joint venture basis.

A fresh tender was called on 15 January 2001 by giving 30 days to submit bids. In response to the NIT, as many as thirteen parties submitted their bids, and after evaluating the various bids by preparing a comparative statement, M/s Asian Housing Construction Ltd (AHCL) was found to be the most suitable and was accordingly recommended by the committee to the cabinet. However, Home Minister Thrang Hok Rangad objected to the recommendation, and the matter was referred to the GAD. On 5 April 2001, the cabinet meeting decided to take the opinions of technical experts, lawyers and chartered accountants, after which the GAD endorsed AHCL and submitted the proposal to the cabinet. Mawlong received the file after the Planning and Finance Departments approved the project. Having full confidence in his ministerial colleagues and officials of the concerned departments, Mawlong gave his approval and the agreement with AHCL was executed on 29 June 2001. Till then, there was no question raised on the soundness of the agreement from any quarters.

The first recorded objection to this deal appeared on 12 October 2001, in an article entitled 'Who is Selling Off Meghalaya's Property in Calcutta' written by Patricia Mukhim in *The*

Shillong Times. In it, the columnist submitted that the deal displays 'corruption at its worst'. Questioning the transparency of the deal, she stated that a junior officer and his seniors 'have done the actual wheeling and dealing'. She alleged that there were many flaws in the agreement and further wrote, 'The people must decide whether Mr EK Mawlong under whose tenure this deal was finalised can still continue in office after such a major scam. It is not as if we are blaming the Chief Minister. We are holding him responsible for throwing away a valuable asset of the state for a pocketful of silver.'

After that, objections began to be raised by ministers within the Government. The Home Minister, Rangad, wrote to Mawlong demanding the constitution of a committee to inquire into the deal. He reiterated that the execution of the Memorandum of Understanding (MoU) didn't have the 'seal of approval' of the Government.

Soon after, the matter was given wide coverage in the media. A flash-in-the-pan group named People's Rally Against Corruption (PRAC), which comprised nine NGOs and pressure groups of which the most prominent were the Khasi Students' Union and Federation of Khasi Jaiñtia and Garo People (FKJGP) demanded that the deal be scrapped and reproached the ones in high office for receiving kickbacks and indulging in blatant corruption. The PRAC, with Rangbah Shnong,

Offlyn Dohling; KSU President, Paul Lyngdoh; FKJGP President, Ardent M Basaïawmoit; and Patricia Mukhim in the forefront, held multiple protest rallies across the city and even held a meeting at Umroi to enlighten the people of the 'corruption' and 'scam' that had transpired. The general public was convinced that Mawlong, his cabinet colleagues and the officers, had 'sold off' the land in Kolkata to the AHCL.[74] However, no FIR or official complaint was filed by the group.

In a nutshell, the deal between the Government and the AHCL was such that the AHCL would incur all expenses for the reconstruction of the Meghalaya House at a cost of Rs 13 crore. After the completion of construction, the completed buildings would be handed over to AHCL for a lease period of 99 years. A joint-venture lease agreement was signed, according to which AHCL would pay the Meghalaya Government Rs 2,50,000 annually. This amount would be raised by Rs 15,000 after every ten years. At the end of the lease period of 99 years, the built-up area comprising the Meghalaya House and the commercial complex would be handed over to the Government of Meghalaya.

Calling this arrangement a 'sell out', the PRAC levelled corruption charges against the Government saying that the lease amount was

74 *'Ka jaidbynriew Khasi ka beh lai lum ïa ki kam pynroi.' Mawphor. 8 December 2003*

highly undervalued. Mukhim and other members of the PRAC questioned the legality of the MoU executed by the Government, and called Mawlong 'the prime architect'[75] of the deal. Mukhim alleged that the Government had skipped protocol as the agreement was never discussed in the cabinet which should have been done before the execution of the deal. The joint venture would incur loss to the state as the Government didn't have the expertise to execute such an agreement and the value of the Kolkata land was highly undervalued.

The columnist wrote that the agreement, 'according to legal experts', not only gave 'undue advantage to the construction firm,' but was also 'unconstitutional'. The then Finance Minister AH Scott Lyngdoh 'claims to have no knowledge of when the deal was finalised'.[76]

In his defense, Mawlong later stated[77] that three Chartered Accounting firms had given their inputs on the deal which were incorporated. The Additional Advocate General's views were sought, and he 'opined that the deal was good.' He clarified that other firms demanded longer lease periods ranging from 99 to 297 years, and castigated AH

75 'Why Meghalaya House deal is not a joint venture', *The Shillong Times, 21 August 2003*

76 'Wanted a public debate on Meghalaya House deal', *The Shillong Times 28 February 2002*

77 ' Mawlong: Nothing wrong with Kolkata deal', *The Shillong Times, 22 February 2002*

Scott Lyngdoh for feigning ignorance over the matter because as Finance Minister he made a file noting, 'This has approval of minister finance'. Refuting the charge that it was a 'sell-out,' he said that the Government would have sole ownership over the land and that it was a 'lease' of the property, not a 'sale.'

The nature of the allegation took its toll on the stability of the coalition Government when the ministers in the Government, particularly Home Minister TH Rangad of the BJP and Martle N Mukhim of the UDP started playing truant. Rangad requested in a letter to the Chief Secretary, who was also the Chairman of the State Vigilance Commission, an investigation by the Anti-Corruption Branch. Ironically, according to Mawlong, Rangad as a member of the Cabinet had approved the same. When Mawlong brought this up on 21 October 2001 in a cabinet meeting at his official residence, Rangad vaguely replied that there were many loopholes and shortcomings in the terms and conditions of the agreement which called for correction and rectification. On being asked to furnish the shortcomings, the latter fumbled and said that he would do so in a future meeting.

More than a week later, during a public rally at Malki Playground, led by the PRAC, under the chairmanship of HP Oflyn Dohling of the Synjuk Ki Rangbah Shnong, the NGO demanded the resignation of Mawlong and Nimarson

Momin within the next 48 hours. Besides, they also demanded the removal of two officers—JP Singh, the Chief Secretary and Arindam Som, the Secretary of the GAD–as perpetrators, and an immediate scrapping of the deal.[78] It stated that it had all the evidence against a few individuals with vested interests who ignored the interest of the people of the state for personal benefit.

The same evening on 29 October, Mawlong convened a Parliamentary Meeting of the UDP and offered to step down if his party colleagues requested the same. However, twenty out of twenty-two legislators were against his resignation as Chief Minister, and vouched their loyalty to him and to the coalition.

The following day, Mawlong received a letter of resignation from Martle N Mukhim as Minister. Despite repeated requests by the Chief Minister, Mukhim refused to withdraw his resignation. On 1 November, Purno A Sangma, General Secretary of the NCP, UDP's coalition partner in the Government rushed to Shillong to manage the political crisis. The visit was highly anticipated as it was a precursor to NCP's decision whether it would continue to extend support to the beleaguered Government.

78 'Rally demands CM's resignation over house deal', *The Meghalaya Guardian, 30 October 2001*

A Cabinet meeting stated for 9 November was preponed to 3 November, and under stiff opposition from members including Rangad and the then Minister of Finance, AH Scott Lyngdoh, Mawlong proposed that the project be withdrawn. The AHCL was informed accordingly. The Cabinet cancelled the whole project on 3 November.

Despite the decision to scrap the entire deal, the PRAC was relentless and continued to demand the resignation of the CM along with their other demands and threatened to continue the agitation until they were met. On 13 November, the PRAC demanded a judicial inquiry be set up headed by a sitting judge of the Gauhati High Court but reiterated that as long as the Chief Minister was in the chair, the PRAC would not accept any report submitted by such an inquiry.

Mawlong agreed to constitute a Commission of Inquiry and requested the Chief Justice of the Gauhati High Court to provide one sitting Judge but no sitting Judge was available for the task and the Chief Justice proposed the names of retired judges. The Government appointed Justice S Haque (retired) as he happened to be the first on the list of the retired judges empaneled by the High Court. Mawlong refused to step down and vowed to fight on.

By then the political situation had taken a turn for the worse. Rangad was stripped of the Home portfolio and this was followed by the resignation

of his BJP colleague Alexander Laloo Hek and withdrawal of the BJP from the Government. Purno A Sangma, the NCP leader and Member of Parliament, directed the NCP MLAs to withdraw support from the Government. However, twelve MLAs of the NCP refused to abide by Purno's directive and split from the parent party under the leadership of Lotsing Sangma to form the Meghalaya Nationalist Congress Legislature Party (MNCLP).[79] But a few days later, fearing disqualification on the grounds of violating the provisions of the Tenth Schedule, the rebels returned to their original party, the NCP.

On 28 November 2001, Mawlong received a major blow when eight UDP legislators split from the parent party and formed the Meghalaya United Democratic Party (MUDP) led by AH Scott Lyngdoh and seven others including BB Lyngdoh, Martle N Mukhim, DP Iangjuh, Simon Siangshai, Process T Sawkmie, Sanbor Swell, and Rasor Rani. Interestingly, the next month, Rangad said in the winter session of the Assembly that he did not blame the Chief Minister for not stepping down. He said the legislators 'were his staunch supporters among the MLAs and his party, encouraging him at every step not to step down and of course the NCP till the last moment.' However, he also added

79 'Rebel NCP MLAs split party, back Mawlong.' *The Meghalaya Guardian. 20 November, 2001.*

that 'they had been supporting the then Chief Minister with false hope and ditched him at the last moment.'

On 7 December, the Assembly witnessed pandemonium when a No-Confidence Motion against the Government was tabled and many legislators in the ruling side objected to the unconstitutional actions of the Speaker, ED Marak of the NCP. The major objection was that sufficient time was not taken to recognise the MUDP as a legislative party and the NCP-led Government-in-waiting was favoured. The No-Confidence Motion was passed through a voice vote, thereby signaling the end of Mawlong's Government.

Mawlong ultimately resigned on 8 December 2001 paving the way for an Independent Legislator, Dr FA Khonglam to take over as Chief Minister. He formed the People's Forum of Meghalaya (PFM) comprising the NCP, the INC, the MUDP and some other Independent MLAs. Purno A Sangma in a press briefing justified the overthrow of the Mawlong-led Government as a reflection of the sentiments of the people, who were restless against the corruption perpetrated in the Meghalaya House Deal.[80]

Following Mawlong's resignation, the PFM Government appointed a one-man Commission

80 'Game up for Mawlong, Purno wins.' *The Meghalaya Guardian. 28 November 2001*

of inquiry headed by Justice SP Rajkhowa, a retired Judge of Calcutta High Court, to probe the allegations against Mawlong, Momin and other officials. The Commission of Inquiry headed by Justice S Haque, thus, died a natural death.

The Rajkhowa Commission started conducting the inquiry in Shillong and asked stakeholders to file their submissions. Ironically, the PRAC didn't depose before the commission.[81] Only Mawlong, Nimarson Momin, JP Singh, Martle Mukhim and Patricia Mukhim appeared before it in their individual capacities. And even before the Commission could complete its task and submit a report, the PRAC accused it of a 'blatantly biased and unprofessional attitude'.[82] It further stated that 'this was evident from the shoddy treatment meted out to the counsels of the petitioners and the Commission's refusal to facilitate a fair trial by denying them access to relevant records and papers.'[83]

Subsequently, the pressure groups, political parties, NGOs, and individual stakeholders withdrew their representations and desisted from appearing before the Rajkhowa Commission.[84]

81 '*Pep ki PRAC sha ka jingtohkit Meghalaya House, leit ai sakhi shimet u Bah EK Mawlong,' Rupang. 1 May 2002*

82 'Rajkhowa Commission is biased, says PRAC' *The Shillong Times, 21 May 2002*

83 *Ibid*

84 '*Lah ban pyndam noh ïa ka Rajkhowa Commission, 42 Lak lut ka Phukan Commission: CM.' Mawphor. 7 August 2002*

The Government also eventually de-notified the Commission before it could submit its report. The Government instead decided to hand over the investigation to the Central Bureau of Investigation 'for the sake of transparency and accountability'.[85]

Mawlong appealed to the Government to revive the Rajkhowa Commission, but his plea was rejected. Calling the move to hand over the investigation to the CBI politically motivated, Mawlong said in a press conference that this was a tactic to target him before the Legislative Assembly elections the next year. Mawlong was supported by SD Khongwir and Bindo Lanong of the UDP and added that while they were not opposed to the CBI inquiry, the Rajkhowa Commission should have been allowed to 'complete the enquiry'.[86] He said:

> The NCP, the Congress, the BJP, NCP leader PA Sangma and the NGOs initially wanted the Meghalaya House deal to be scrapped and the deal was scrapped. Later they asked for the enquiry and that too was initiated by the Government and what more did they want?...Let the findings of the commission be out and if the Government is not happy, they can decide the future course of action.

85 'Cabinet may hand over Kolkata deal probe to CBI,' *The Shillong Times, 2 August 2002*

86 'CBI probe 'politically motivated: Mawlong.' *The Shillong Times, 8 August 2002*

He stated that his intention was to generate more income for the state through the deal and the people who opposed the deal should be held responsible since they did not understand the benefits. He questioned the attitude of those who 'on the one hand wanted development and on the other, opposed any move for more investment and progress.'[87]

Throughout the drama that played out for over six months, Mawlong lamented his inability to clarify his stand on the floor of the Assembly on the day when the No-Confidence Motion was tabled against his Government. Another regret was that *The Shillong Times* refused to publish the two articles written by him to clarify the facts about the Meghalaya House issue, which were later published by *The Meghalaya Guardian* in August 2002. He also published his clarification, written in English and Khasi, on pamphlets which were widely distributed to the general public. The man who had brought together three regional parties with other leaders to form the UDP, was naturally distressed over the politicisation of the entire issue and also the unreconciled bitterness with his one-time college friend, Purno A Sangma, whom the UDP later blamed for 'acting as a catalyst in overthrowing the EK Mawlong Government'.[88]

87 *Ibid*

88 'UDP blames Purno for Mawlong's exit', *The Shillong Times, 22 February 2002*

Mawlong too felt betrayed because as Speaker of the Legislative Assembly, he had prevented a probable disqualification of a bunch of NCP MLAs who had split from the Congress as a favour to his friend. The seesaw eventually came to a distasteful end for Mawlong; clearly manifesting the brutishness of political games in the cloudscape of Meghalaya politics.

On 19 December 2002, the PRAC submitted a memorandum to the Chief Minister FA Khonglam claiming to commit itself to 'fight all forms of corruption in governance and administration.' It further claimed that the agreement was 'an open and shut case of criminal conspiracy' between the former Government and the aforesaid company and sacrificed the 'economic interests of the state.' The decision to scrap the Meghalaya House deal, they said was evidence for the fact that the deal was not in conformity with the rules of conduct of business of the Government of Meghalaya.

Defining PRAC's fight against corruption as an enduring agenda, Patricia Mukhim wrote in an article:

> I have repeatedly said that fighting corruption is not a short-term goal but a long-term agenda and those in the fight cannot get cynical. There are those who would like to deflect the attention of the PRAC by accusing it of not taking up other issues of corruption. To such the answer is–one step at a time. Agreed, there

> are several burning issues in the state. But there are also other groups, individuals and organisations who can share the burden instead of pointing accusing fingers at those who have taken at least one issue to its logical end.

The irony perhaps many had noticed was that the Kolkata deal was the first and only issue that the PRAC ever took up so earnestly, and subsequently faded into oblivion.

After much of the dust settled down, Mawlong decided to lay low, particularly after his loss in the 2003 election. The unexpected election result was a rude shock to him and his supporters. He spent most of his time at home, but as it had been customary for people to drop in for more than three decades, the outcome of the election didn't change that routine. Following his loss, he resigned as President of the UDP in April 2003. He was appointed Chairman of the State Development Reforms Commission by the incumbent Government, and was frequently engrossed with work related to it.

He was determined to remove the stigma on his name. He would often overtly express to visitors at his Lower Mawprem home that he was accused of corruption without any proof. The leaders of the PRAC, according to him, could have sought clarification from the Government over the MoU signed with the AHCL, and that approach would have been more civil. Instead, they took recourse to

theatrics and slogan shouting.

The passage of the Right to Information Act (RTI) in the Indian Parliament in 2005, though, allowed him to absolve himself. The Commission of Inquiry had been scrapped and the progress of the CBI investigation was delayed because neither an FIR nor a complaint was filed against Mawlong.

In the RTI, he sought relevant documents from the Political Department regarding the alleged sale of the Meghalaya House property. However, to his utter dismay, the next month, on 14 September 2006, the Public Information Officer, said that he was 'directed to inform that the Government has received no information from the CBI so far.'

Irked by the one-liner, he reminded the GAD and Political Departments that the deal led to a huge outcry which ultimately led to his ouster as Chief Minister of Meghalaya. Hence, it was necessary to provide him 'the entire details as to when and how the CBI inquiry was initiated against the alleged deal and subsequent follow up action taken by the State Government.' In the letter he reasoned:

> A CBI inquiry was sought to be initiated as party to the purportedly illegal deal. Even though subsequent governments arrived at a settlement with M/s Asian Housing and Construction Private Limited, the action of the Government prior to the said settlement has cast a stigma against my name and my reputation.'

The AHCL came to an understanding with the Government that it would construct the Meghalaya House at Russell Street at a cost of Rs 22 crore after a meeting in Kolkata on 21-22 April 2004.[89] As the AHCL had approached the Calcutta High Court after the first MoU was cancelled, the Government and the company agreed for an out-of-court settlement, and a fresh MoU was signed.

It had been four years since the case was handed over to the CBI on 19 December 2002. But there was no satisfactory reply. However, even till 14 November 2006, 'the Political Department had again sought for information from the Secretary, Government of India with regard to its decision on the transfer of the case to the CBI.'

It became evident that the case was held up due to meaningless communication between the Centre and the State Governments, with no conclusive end in sight. In April 2007, Mawlong filed a writ petition in the Shillong bench of the Guwahati High Court against the Government of Meghalaya to clear his name from the alleged scam.

89 'Govt, AHCL reach understanding' *The Shillong Times, 27 April 2004*

INTEGRITY UPHELD

IT WAS an unusually busy and noisy morning. Men and women, mostly from Umroi had converged in the compound of Mawlong's household on 28 January 2008, eager to celebrate his impending candidature in the forthcoming February election. Angelina Riasida Lyngdoh, a stout and busy woman who had been a strong pillar of support to her husband, kept glancing at the clock but couldn't wriggle out. That was her thirty-first year of entertaining guests at home, while her politician-husband patiently listened to the needs of his constituents. She had to leave for the court hearing, and the guests had to be served refreshments. At about quarter to ten, she was sure she could not get out. She told George, her eldest son, to go to the court instead of his workplace. Mawlong was in the verandah, wrapped in a Naga shawl to keep the January chill at bay. Seated on a cane chair, he seemed preoccupied as it was yet another day of hearing at the court. Surrounded by his confidants PK Lynser and Babu Dwik Kharkongor, he asked rhetorically, 'I wonder what the Judge will do today. Would he set another date or pass a judgement? Whatever be the decision, we have to focus on the election, and we will campaign diligently.'

When the cordless telephone rang thirty minutes later, his wife answered the call and was relieved to hear the familiar and excited voice. *'Mei, i Pa i la jop!'* (Mother, father is victorious!) George said.

Recalling that moment vividly, Angelina Riasida narrated that with a heart full of indescribable emotion, she skipped to the veranda to break the news to her husband. She bent forward and hugged him while conveying the message that the court had cleared his name of any wrongdoing in the Kolkata Meghalaya House Deal. At first, Mawlong didn't react or say a single word. After a brief silent pause, he simply bowed his head and broke down uncontrollably, his wife recalled. Mawlong's friends and well-wishers who were present in different rooms and outside the house rushed towards the veranda when they heard the news. It was the first time that they witnessed their leader in tears. It became evident that Mawlong had carried an enormous emotional weight for seven years. The people around shook hands and hugged one another in joy, and moved closer to console their

leader to celebrate the victory instead. Feeling his spirits restored, Mawlong instructed his wife to call each of his children to return home immediately after work. The family spent a memorable evening together, bowing in prayer and thanking God for the favourable verdict.

In his judgement, Judge T Vaiphei of the Honourable Guwahati High Court raised an alarm that it was an unusual Writ Petition. There was neither an FIR nor an ongoing criminal proceeding. Instead, the CBI was simply directed to investigate whether a person has committed an offence. He said that this was against the rights of life and liberty guaranteed under Article 21 of the Indian Constitution. He ruled:

> Right to Life, set out in Article 21, means something more than mere survival or animal existence. This right also includes the right to live with human dignity…A man has, therefore, to be let alone to enjoy 'LIFE' without fetters. He cannot be hounded by the police of CBI merely to find out whether he has committed any offence or is living as a law-abiding citizen.

Notwithstanding the magnitude of corruption prevalent in the country, the Judge expressed his difficulty in visualising that an agreement entered with a company could have been done under 'suspicious circumstances' or could be stated that 'there had been kickbacks' when the project had

already been examined and approved by different statutory and other Government agencies. Starting a criminal investigation on a 'crime unknown' and on 'mere conjecture' or 'flight of fancy' cannot be termed reasonable. He called it akin to firing a shot in the dark without even knowing if there was a prey at all, thereby creating 'sound and fury' but without achieving any substantial result.

The Judge reasoned that it would not be expedient to direct the CBI to conduct an investigation into a matter 'in the absence of definite materials against the petitioner…it will be unfair, vexatious as well as illegal on the part of the State-respondents.'

Calling for a fine balance between the fundamental rights of a citizen and power of the police to investigate a cognisable offence, the Judge said that the powers of investigation do not warrant 'subjecting a citizen to investigation and the consequential harassment, mental agony and loss of reputation'. For five years, the authorities have resorted to 'half-baked action' or 'a series of correspondences exchanged between the State Government and the Ministry of Personnel, Government of India without tangible results'. This keeps the 'petitioner in the lurch'.

> He is neither here nor there. Perhaps, the initial euphoria has apparently died down. This is only natural when public memory is proverbially short. On the other hand, the petitioner is unable to prove his innocence

> or is being successfully prosecuted due to the half-hearted action taken by the authorities. Therefore, there is considerable force in the grievances projected by the petitioner. For the reasons stated in the foregoing, I have no alternative but to allow the writ petition.

The Judge asked the state not to pursue the letter written by the State Government to the Government of India on 19 December 2006. He added that if the state or concerned persons find appropriate material, it must be placed before any investigating agency including the CBI to register a case and investigate the matter.

The judgement was termed 'significant for several reasons'[90] as the infamous charge against Mawlong was 'only to hound him out of public office because that was the easiest option available to his detractors, particularly the Nationalist Congress Party (NCP).' The charges were proved 'frivolous' and 'politically motivated' because there was no serious pursuit of the so-called investigation. The Government didn't send reminders to the CBI or the Government of India after the first communication was made on 19 December 2002. The alleged scandal had hit headlines in almost the entire North-East because it concerned an allegation against a Chief Minister. A worrying factor was the

90 Editorial, *The Meghalaya Guardian*, 30 January 2008

manifestation of a 'culture of political vendetta and unabashed display of greed and power' which led to the manufacturing of frivolous but grave allegations.

The opinion reinforced what Mawlong had often said to Babu Dwik Kharkongor and other supporters. He saw the entire episode as a proxy political game because his Government was steadily gaining the goodwill of the people through its positive initiatives. Bringing the UDP down at any cost was the only option available to his political detractors if they wanted to succeed in the 2003 election. There were also rumours that certain business and mining lobbies wanted to topple his Government as Mawlong was not a leader who could be easily influenced. The Meghalaya House scandal provided them with the perfect opportunity to dislodge the Government.

Former UDP Legislator PT Sawkmie, who was closely associated with Mawlong as a UDP Legislator, but later quit the party in 2001 to form the MDP, said in an interview that the scandal was a 'non-issue'. Mawlong was supported in the cabinet on the deal but 'some manipulative elements who wanted to build their own reputation at Mawlong's expense, took advantage.' Besides, 'there were a few senior leaders who aspired to take his place', he added.

Another factor was Bah Mawlong's style of functioning itself. He could not be

> easily dictated by outside forces. He never entertained businessmen. All said and done, it was an unfavourable time for him to govern. Unlike now, the mind-set of people then was very narrow. Nobody bothered to ascertain the facts from the Government before reaching a conclusion.

Even HDR Lyngdoh of the INC believes that 'Bah Mawlong was clean. He was innocent.'

> The problem is most times the public gets excited very quickly over something they know little about, but that excitement and enthusiasm never lasts long. People accused him of corruption and called him names, and that condemnation must have affected him mentally and physically. At the end of the day, he remains in my memory as one of the best parliamentarians the state has ever had. A jolly and hearty person who was an efficient statesman, and his activeness in questioning and giving suggestions to the Government earned him the name Ex-Facto Leader of the Opposition.

The Kolkata Meghalaya House deal controversy that ultimately led to the downfall of his Government and a loss of reputation, was the most displeasing episode for Mawlong during his long and illustrious career. The favourable judgement, however, effaced the unwarranted stigma.

THE FAITHFUL LAITY

(Co-authored with Emdorini Thangkhiew, Assistant Professor, Department of Political Science, Synod College, Shillong)

LOCAL CHURCH bodies and various social organisations have contributed largely to the development of the state since its inception in 1972, particularly in Human Resource. European and American Christian Missionaries conquered the hazardous terrain of the state, and propagated both formal education as well as, the Christian faith among the tribal masses since before independence. The Christian missionaries were the pioneers of modern education in the Khasi, Jaiñtia, and Garo Hills. Shillong, which is considered to be one of the best places for education in the North-East, owes much of its distinction to the missionaries–particularly the Catholic missions–who established illustrious schools and colleges in the beautiful pine city in the early twentieth century. In fact, the formulation of the Khasi Alphabet in 1842 is attributed to Reverend Thomas Jones, a Welsh Presbyterian missionary. Similarly, in the Garo

Hills, the American Baptist missionaries used the Roman script and a Garo Alphabet was evolved in 1902.

Despite being a small community in India, the Catholic Church has contributed largely by way of setting up educational institutions throughout the country. The first historically recorded contact that the church made with the North-Eastern states of India was when two Jesuit missionaries, John Cebral and Stephen Cacella visited Assam in 1627 on their way to Tibet.[91] Thereafter, small communities of foreign priests visited the North-East, but very few stayed long. It was only after the establishment of the Prefecture Apostolic of Assam of the Society of the Divine Saviour in 1890[92] popularly known as the 'Salvatorians', a society which specialised in Catholic Education, that the Catholic mission could begin its work earnestly. Fr Otto Hopfenmüller was appointed the first Apostolic Prefect of the Prefecture on 13 December 1889 and Shillong was chosen as the main place of operation.

The Salvatorian fathers worked tirelessly and trained their personnel in the teaching profession. They established schools in Shillong, Raliang, Sohra (Cherrapunjee), and Guwahati. Along with their Christian mission, they involved themselves

91 Varghese, Pius, *School Education in Meghalaya–Catholic Contribution, Akansha Publishing House, New Delhi, 2009, pp. 22*

92 *Ibid*

in publishing Christian literature and opened the first printing press in Laitryngew near Sohra in the year 1900. It was later shifted to Shillong and thus enabled the Don Bosco Technical School to start the press, which stands till today. The fathers published many books in the Khasi language too.

The Salvatorian fathers started St. Anthony's Primary School in 1901 initially as an orphanage. However, the outcome of the First World War compelled the German priests to leave the region and their educational mission was continued by the Jesuit Missionaries who stayed from 1915 to 1921. The Jesuit Missionaries were succeeded by the Salesian priests also known as the Don Bosco Fathers and Brothers who reached Shillong in 1922. The Salesian fathers also took over St Anthony's School, and since then have been providing quality education in the remotest corners of the Khasi, Jaiñtia and Garo Hills.

It was under the guidance of the Salesian priests, whose mandate is not only impart knowledge but also to serve and to be responsible for others, that EK Mawlong and many other prominent personalities of the Khasi-Jaiñtia and Garo Hills benefitted largely. Like him, there were countless past pupils who continued to maintain cordial relations with the clergy and laity of the church, long after they had passed out from the renowned school and college. His participation in the activities of the Catholic church, other Christian

denominations and social organisations propelled his popularity further.

Mawlong's association with the church started as a member of the Catholic Management Committee in Laitumkhrah, along with Dr S Loniak Marbaniang, when he was a young college student. Thereafter, he dedicated his time to religious and social activities of the Church as an active member of the Don Bosco Past Pupils' Association, Shillong; and the Catholic Association of Khasi and Jaiñtia Hills (CAKJH), Shillong, also known as the Catholic Association of Shillong, an organisation of the Catholic laity endorsed and recognised by the Church. In the year 1975, a group of thirty-three people unanimously decided to start the CAKJH, with the consent and blessings of the Most Reverend Hubert D'Rosario, SDB, DD, the Archbishop of Shillong-Guwahati. Mawlong, then an MDC, was one of the founding members. He was also part of the Central Executive Committee from 1975 to 1977. He was later elected as its President in 1989 succeeding John Deng Pohrmen, till he voluntarily gave up the post in the year 2006, after being its longest serving head for almost 17 years.

In his capacity as the President of the Association, he often offered his assistance whenever called to do so. On 8 March 1987, when the Cathedral of the Risen Lord at Diphu, Karbi Anglong District was blessed, he was a special invitee Speaker of the

Meghalaya Legislative Assembly and President of the CAKJH. On the memorable occasion, Rev Father John Timung, the first Karbi priest was also ordained. Never one to miss an opportunity, Mawlong grabbed the chance and convened a meeting of the Karbi political leaders to discuss the restoration of peaceful co-existence between the Karbis of Assam and the Khasi-Pnars in the disputed Blocks I and II as the two communities often clashed, largely due to the unresolved inter-state boundary issue.

Many a times, he functioned as a peacemaker to calm tempers that often flared up due to various disputes. The role suited him well for he rarely lost his composure except when extremely provoked. In 1987, at Tieh Nongbah village in the West Khasi Hills, there was simmering discontent between the Roman Catholics and the Presbyterian faithful over a Government grant to build a new Middle English School in the village. To resolve the misunderstanding, Mawlong invited leaders of both faiths: Hoping Stone Lyngdoh, MLA, who was also an Elder of the Presbyterian Church, and Fr Luke, Parish Priest of Mairang Parish. Mawlong moderated over the meeting and all the differences could be settled amicably.

There was another case of land dispute that arose between the Khasi Indigenous Faith and the Roman Catholic Church regarding the ownership of a particular plot of land at Umñiuh Pynursla

in 1991 but Mawlong was able to amicably restore peace. Similar situations occurred in Kbet Nongbri, Ri Bhoi District (1976); Sakwang, near Mawkyrwat (1983); Nongum, near Mairang (1984-85); Dokmoka and Diphu, Karbi Anglong District, Assam (1987); Saitsama and Khliehriat, Jaiñtia Hills District (1993); Wahra, near Mairang (1993-1994) and other instances where clashes were prevented and cordially resolved because of his timely intervention.

Fr Sylvanus Nongkynrih, a close associate of the leader, recalled how Mawlong came to the aid of the church when a dispute arose in Umñiuh-Tmar village and another occasion at Mawkhar-Krang in Marbisu Parish, when he was the Parish Priest. Fr Nongkynrih narrated that Mawlong convened a meeting with the villagers and in his signature style, patiently explained the intentions of the church and cleared all their doubts. In 1997, a problem arose at Mawkhar-Krang and most of the complainants happened to be his extended relatives of the Mawlong clan. There again he clarified the church's stance to his nephews and nieces and Fr Nongkynrih witnessed the high regard they had for him.

Prior to the Golden Jubilee Celebration of Marbisu Parish, the villagers of Mawlyngkut were deeply disheartened. Most of them had renovated their homes in anticipation of the grand celebrations, but their homes were yet to be lit up as there was no

transformer and electricity supply. They were living in total darkness. Fr Nongkynrih led a delegation to plead with Mawlong in March 2000 when he became the Chief Minister. He listened patiently to their plea. By June of that year, the village shone brightly at night as light bulbs illuminated the houses at Mawlyngkut. It was indeed a blessing to the people. Mawlong contributed greatly to the Golden Jubilee Celebration of Marbisu Parish in January 2000, and to the Fifth Convention of the Archdiocesan Catholic Youth League (ACYL) which was held in the premises of the parish, recalled Fr Nongkynrih.

Diocesan Administrator of the Shillong Archdiocese, Father John Madur recalls an incident in which he realised Mawlong's virtues of humility, honesty and ability to listen to advice. As the Chief Minister, Mawlong was invited to be the Chief Guest at a function in Don Bosco, Guwahati. 'While the clergy and other guests were waiting expectedly for him to show up in a large convoy of vehicles along with armed bodyguards,' everyone was taken by surprise when he turned up in a local taxi. He happened to be in the city for his check-up, but didn't use any Government vehicle. After the function, he again returned in an auto rickshaw. He was not a fussy person and preferred to get things done quietly and quickly.'

In the year 2006 when Mawlong wasn't keeping well, Fr John Madur visited him at his residence

at Lower Mawprem with another priest. While entering the house, he noticed that there was a half-made building adjacent to the main house. It appeared as though its construction had begun long ago, but had been abandoned for many years. When Fr John inquired about it, Mawlong told him that he had planned to expand the house as he wanted both his daughters to stay together. As they were very close, Fr John had the gumption to ask, 'Why don't you complete it quickly then Bah Heh?' He smiled and quietly replied, 'Father, I don't have money.' Fr John was stumped and at that moment his faith in Mawlong's honesty was further strengthened.

Sometime in 2004, after the untimely death of TH Rangad, Mawlong called upon Fr John at Laban when he was its Parish Priest. Mawlong confided to Fr John that there were some individuals who were advising him to contest the bye-election from Laban following TH Rangad's death. After he had lost the General Election from Umroi in 2003, he told Fr John that he couldn't simply sit idle after being in public service for so long. Fr John was troubled by the news because he honestly felt it wasn't a good prospect. For about three hours, along with other friends, they brainstormed over the issue and Fr John tried his best to reason with him about the impending pitfall of such a move. After listening to all sides, Mawlong finally relented. 'Due to his humility, he listened to my advice, and heeded the

guidance of those who wanted the best for him,' concluded Fr John Madur.

His two stints as Speaker of the Meghalaya Legislative Assembly, and once as Chief Minister, enabled him to travel beyond the shores of the country to visit other nations as the State's representative. He travelled to Nairobi, Kenya in 1983 for a Commonwealth Parliamentary Association Conference. He visited Cairo, Egypt; London, United Kingdom; Frankfurt, Germany; and Rome, Italy. He attended the Commonwealth Parliamentary Association Conference in Kuala Lumpur, Malaysia in 1987, and also travelled to Bangkok, Thailand; Tokyo, Japan; and Singapore. The third time he attended the Commonwealth Parliamentary Association Conference was in New Zealand in 1998 after which he went to New York, USA and Amsterdam in the Netherlands.

While in Rome in 1983, he met his Holiness Pope John Paul II in the Vatican. In his cordial meeting with the Pope who bestowed his Papal Blessing upon him and his family, he took the opportunity to invite him to visit his hometown, Shillong. Steadfast and dedicated as he was, he realised his dream of making the Papal Visit a success on February 4, 1986. However, the dream was realised after a lot of hard work.

In a write-up to commemorate the twentieth anniversary of the Papal Visit of Pope John Paul II published in *Ka Ïing Khristan*[93] in February 2006, Mawlong recounted the endless difficulties he faced in the attempt to bring the Pope to Shillong.

As soon as the news of the Pope's impending visit to India spread, the Catholic Bishops' Conference of India (CBCI) met to plan out the places that His Holiness could visit. Bishops across the country tried to get him to their Archdiocese and Diocese. The Catholic leaders and elders of the church in Shillong too persuaded the Archbishop of the Archdiocese, the Most Reverend Hubert D'Rosario to try his best in keeping Shillong as one of the places. Being a respectable figure, Archbishop Hubert succeeded in convincing the CBCI. By the time the meeting of the CBCI got over, it was late at night. But due to the urgency of the matter, the Archbishop made a telephone call to the man whom he thought would be the best to entrust the first and most important assignment. He dialled Mawlong's number and told him to meet immediately. In the meeting, the Archbishop requested Mawlong, who was the Speaker of the Legislative Assembly at that time, to leave for New Delhi and negotiate on behalf of Shillong. In New Delhi, he was told by the Archbishop, to speak with the Protocol Officer in the Ministry of External Affairs, who was known to be a 'hard nut'. Archbishop Hubert said, 'I know

93 A monthly Christian magazine published by the Shillong Archdiocese

you will not let me down.' With the Archbishop's blessings, he left for the capital for a two-week long and agonising stay.

When Mawlong reached New Delhi, he was happy to learn that the Chief Minister, Captain Williamson A Sangma, was also there. The next morning, he went to the Chief Minister and explained the purpose of his visit. He requested Captain Sangma to accompany him to meet the Union Home Minister, SB Chavan. Captain Sangma's immediate comment was that he was not a Catholic, to which Mawlong replied that the Pope himself was visiting more in his capacity as a Head of State, and less as the Head of the Catholic Faith.

Upon agreeing, they together met the Union Home Minister who convinced them that he would take up the matter with the concerned persons.

Not satisfied with what he had accomplished, Mawlong reached out to another influential friend from Meghalaya, a Cabinet Minister in Rajiv Gandhi's Government and a long-time friend, Purno A Sangma. After explaining the purpose to Sangma, they fixed an appointment with the Prime Minister, Rajiv Gandhi. The very next day, accompanied by Sangma, Mawlong met Rajiv Gandhi to explain the great aspiration of the Catholic faithful of the entire North-East to meet and greet the Holy Father, Pope John Paul II. Rajiv Gandhi was receptive of their desire and promised to lend his help. The only problem, he explained,

was with the Ministry of Home Affairs which could be a little strict with the programme due to security concerns. After promising to help, he saw them out. The days rolled by, without much hope in sight.

Every evening, back in his room in the Meghalaya House in New Delhi, he would call Shillong to inform the Archbishop of the day's progress. A little more hopeful than the previous days, he informed the Archbishop that he had two more meetings with the Minister of External Affairs and the Protocol Officer. Again he sought the help of Purno A Sangma to set a meeting with the Minister of State, Ministry of External Affairs, Khurshid Alam Khan, who later directed them to meet the Protocol Officer, whom the Archbishop had described as a 'hard nut'. The two friends went to the Protocol Officer's room and stated their desire to add Shillong to the Tour Programme (Itinerary) of the Holy See. They informed that Shillong was chosen as the only venue in the whole of North-East India, which included the Seven Sister States with a large Christian population. At that point, the officer interrupted them and highlighted the many problems of adding a remote town like Shillong to the itinerary, especially with regards to security. In response, Mawlong assured him that nothing untoward will ever happen as the people had high regard for the Holy Father. He also guaranteed that the Government machinery would

work round-the-clock to ensure that the police and the public would act responsibly.

A 'hard nut' that he was, the Protocol Officer was still not convinced and showed his hesitation. At that point, the usually calm Mawlong lost his patience, and showing his frustration he said, 'It is this kind of attitude that you people in the mainland have for the North-East, and the common deprecating perception that has been created about us, that has produced, and will continue to produce, a strong sense of mental distance between the North-East and the rest of India.' Perhaps tickled and stung by what he said, the Protocol Officer finally conceded and agreed to put Shillong in the Pope's itinerary. However, he dictated that it was to be only for a short duration of three hours due to security concerns. The two bargained with the officer for more time so that the Pope could at least eat with them, and halt a night in Shillong. Despite their efforts, the officer was adamant and not keen on changing the programme any further. For two hours, Mawlong and Sangma sat with the officer to change his mind, but after realising that he would not budge any further, they reluctantly accepted his decision. They acceded that 'A done something is better than a perfect nothing'. Disheartened, they left his chamber with a final request to intimate them if there was a possibility of extending the visit.

Both Mawlong and Purno Sangma thought of other ways in order to get permission for a longer

stay for the Pope. In the end, they decided that it was better to have him for a few hours than to run the risk of losing the visit entirely. Mawlong decided not to pursue it any further and to count the little blessings.

After many days in New Delhi, he finally had some good news for the Archbishop. Upon reaching his room, he called the Archbishop to inform him about the final decision and narrated how he, along with Purno A Sangma, tried their best to convince the Protocol Officer. It was difficult, however, because it was the Ministry of External Affairs that arranged and coordinated the entire programme of the Pope's visit to India, and the Protocol officer was indeed a tough man. Thereafter, Mawlong returned home.

A few days later, the Archbishop received official information from the Government of India that the programme of the Pope had been fixed for 4 February 1986 in Shillong. Immediately, preparations were then made to welcome the Pope. A number of meetings were held at the Archbishop's House and different committees were formed, and the picturesque Golf Links was selected as the venue as they anticipated an enormous crowd would visit the capital city. The preparation of the podium at the scenic Golf Links in Shillong was truly grand and splendid. Every tiny detail was checked twice and made sure that nothing was overlooked. Never did Shillong ever witness such a grand preparation

for the momentous Papal visit.

It was truly an unforgettable visit for those who witnessed the once-in-a-lifetime event. It was a historical moment not just for the Catholic Church of the state, but for the entire country as well. People camped the night before the Pope's arrival just to get front seats to see the Pope. Mawlong, who was then residing in the Government quarters near Ward's Lake, could hear vehicles big and small with people singing and cheering joyfully as they drove down the road from Polo to Golf Links. The sound of the singing crowd and endless stream of vehicles went on the entire night till the next morning.

One such troupe was from Nagaland. Accompanied by their priest, Fr Jesudah Fernando, some faithful of the Konyak tribe of Nagaland, who carried their bright attires, sarongs, and long curved sabres, had travelled four days by truck, train and bus just to attend the Holy Mass. By eight in the morning, the number of people at Golf Links had almost reached lakhs. People of all tribes, language and colour converged together to witness the event. The Golf Links resonated as voices rejoiced in joyful hymns, as the people eagerly awaited the arrival of the Holy Father.

On the designated time at 9 am, Pope John Paul II landed in a helicopter at Upper Shillong where he was welcomed by the Archbishop, Bishops of all the dioceses of the North-East, clergy, political leaders, and prominent members of the church including Mawlong. The compassionate Pope shook every hand that was extended towards him. Thereafter, he was escorted amidst tight security, to the picturesque Golf Links for the Holy Mass. As soon as his feet touched the glamorous podium, the place reverberated with people's cheers and specially made Vatican flags waved above their heads. This was followed by songs of praise and worship. The Pope with a thankful heart, waved and smiled at the over joyous congregation.

A short cultural programme was also put up where the diverse traditions and cultures of the people of India were displayed. The Pope sat on a raised platform with tribal dancers surrounding him. In his message the Pope encouraged the Church to strengthen the diverse culture of the people. He also spoke about the role and responsibility of the youth to build and strengthen the Church. In his homily, the Pope, who spoke in English, praised the 'countless courageous priests' and other religious workers who braved 'innumerable difficulties and obstacles of every kind, even to the extent of shedding their blood' to bring Christianity to this region. He also said, 'The future of the Church sits in the hands of you the youth. Live a good life with respect for God and people; be a light to others.'

After the conclusion of the Holy Mass, the Pope thanked the people as he prepared to depart. The people were terribly disappointed by the short time

that was allotted, yet they gave him a warm applause waving their flags with a heavy heart, and many had tears in their eyes. Pope John Paul II left Shillong, and it remains uncertain as to when an incumbent Pope will ever step foot in these parts again.

Mawlong worked whole-heartedly for the cause of the various organisations of the Church. The Divine Saviour Higher Secondary School, Laitumkhrah, which caters especially to the poor and needy students, saw improvements in the infrastructure when Mawlong was the CM. When the Don Bosco Past Pupils' Association, Turin, Italy celebrated its centenary year in 1970, he contributed substantially to the celebrations which were commemorated in Shilong as well.

In his capacity as Chief Minister and President of the Catholic Association, he contributed immensely to the two-day Annual Meet of the All India Catholic Union (AICU) which was organised by the Don Bosco Youth Centre, Laitumkhrah in 2000. Delegates from all parts of India participated and were very satisfied with the arrangements made during the two days. In the closing function, the Archbishop of the Shillong Archdiocese, Most Reverend Dominic Jala remarked, 'We are indeed fortunate to have in our midst, the Chief Minister of the State of Meghalaya, who is a Catholic.' When his turn to speak came, the hall resonated with laughter after the witty Mawlong quipped, 'We are also very fortunate to be graced by the presence of

the Archbishop of the Shillong Archdiocese, who like me, is also a Catholic.'

As President of the Catholic Association, he organised a Peace Rally on 12 December 1998 at the Fire Brigade Field (Madan Ïew Rynghep), Laitmukhrah. The rally's objective was to protest against the attacks, atrocities, and heinous crimes perpetrated on Christians and other minorities in India. The burning alive of an Australian Christian Missionary, Graham Staines, more than 22 years ago, with his two sons inside their vehicle in Orissa triggered widespread condemnation. The Catholic Association in Shillong joined the chorus by raising a peaceful protest at the Jawaharlal Nehru Stadium, Polo Ground, Shillong, in January 1999. Besides Church leaders of various denominations who addressed the meeting, the Lok Sabha MP from Shillong, PR Kyndiah, highlighted the spirit of secularism as enshrined in the Constitution.

Fellow member in the Catholic Association, Billy P Domes opined that Mawlong was 'not only Catholic by faith, but also Catholic in his approach and outlook' because in his own way he reached out to the faithful of other denominations and faiths. For instance, he was troubled and visibly distraught when the Khasi-Jaiñtia Presbyterian Synod Hospital in Jowai was destroyed in a massive fire in 2000. The people grieved the loss of the hospital. To show his solidarity Mawlong met with the hospital administration and offered them financial assistance

for the reconstruction of the hospital.

As a secularist, his affection extended to all in Meghalaya, including the believers across all religions, be it any other Christian denomination, or those of the Khasi indigenous faith, Hinduism, Islam, or Sikhism. Whenever he could, he attended important religious functions across all faiths. He shared a good rapport with the settlers at the Harijan Colony, one of who was Bilu Singh, an employee in the Lake House when he was the Speaker. He was a frequent invitee to commemorate significant festivals like Guru Nanak Jayanti in the Harijan Colony at Ïew Mawlong.

As a family man, he instilled a sense of discipline pertaining to regularity in attending Sunday Mass, praying together as a family before bed, and often took his children to innumerable village parishes on special occasions. Notwithstanding the condition of the roads, he travelled to the nook and corners of Khasi and Jaiñtia Hills to partake in Eucharistic processions, blessing of new parishes or churches, priestly ordinations, and conventions of the various organisations of the Church. As a devout Catholic, his love and deep attachment for the Church manifested in his active contribution and participation. As a statesman, he reached out to all and sundry to render his service in his capacity as a responsible leader of the state.

THE LAST TRIUMPH

IN KHASI culture, there are traditional dance forms called *Shad Suk Mynsiem* and *Shad Pomblang* in which the male dancers sling a quiver or *ka ryngkap* on their back that holds together three arrows. The arrows, the Khasi elders say, are symbolic of the central responsibilities that are bestowed upon *U Rangbah* or an adult male for as long as he lives. The arrows stand for three important institutions: *ka ïing ka sem* or the conjugal family, *ka kur ka jait* or the consanguine family and the clan as a whole, and *ka Ri bad ka jaidbynriew* or the domicile state and its people.

It is believed that a responsible individual is one who, despite having a conjugal family, does not set aside his consanguine roots and also strives to work for the welfare of his community and the people at large. When a man dances to the beat of *ka nakra* or the traditional drum in a traditional dance, he holds a ceremonial sword in one hand

and a cluster of a horsetail whisk in the other as props. While the sword symbolises the warrior, the whisk stands for tranquillity. The ancient Khasi, therefore, spoke of the need to possess a balanced personality in order to live a meaningful life–a life that is not self-centred but one that is sensitive towards the requirements of siblings, relatives and the entire community.

Throughout his adult life, EK Mawlong strove to accomplish these goals.

Mawlong met his wife, Angelina Riasida Lyngdoh Mawphlang, in 1975 during his visits to Sentina Lyngdoh's place. Sentina, fondly called Duh[94] Sen, was Mawlong's close associate and ardent supporter, and her husband, an engineer in the Meghalaya State Electricity Board (MeSEB), stayed in one of the staff quarters along with her family located at Umïam. Angelina, fondly called Ria, stayed in one of the quarters with her maternal aunt Sylvannah Lyngdoh Mawphlang, a schoolteacher in the High School run by the MeSEB.

Ria was close to Duh Sentina as they already had a long family association. Originally from Jaïaw in Shillong, Ria was born on 14 June 1957 to Princila Lyngdoh Mawphlang and P Nongkynrih. As her mother passed away when she was very

94 Duh, the shorter version of Khat Duh, means the youngest among siblings

young, Ria grew up under the foster care of her maternal aunts: Klotida, Lucia Klinibon, Delina, and Sylvannah, the youngest of all. She spent her teenage and young adult life mostly with Delina and Sylvannah.

Ria's grandmother, Khrehsibon Lyngdoh Mawphlang, a resident of Jaïaw fondly called Mei Jaïaw, was a midwife well-known for her expertise in prescribing herbal medication to expecting mothers. Since access to modern medical care was difficult and costly for the marginalised, she was able to touch many lives in those days. Duh Sen was one of those who was touched by the helping hands of Mei Jaïaw. Owing to the close acquaintance she had with her grandmother, Duh Sen treated Ria as her own child.

While Mawlong and Ria fostered a romantic attachment gradually, as he slowly gained her confidence, the hesitant young woman told him to speak directly with her relatives if he really intended to carry the relationship forward.

Eminiency Lyngdoh Mawphlang, a first cousin of Ria, vividly recalls the events that led to their marriage. Like all well-meaning relatives, they wanted the best for Ria, whom everybody loved dearly. When Ria told them about Mawlong's intentions, they were eager to find out more about him. As he was from Mawmih, an obscure village, they inquired from people who knew more about him like his landlady at Mission Compound and

Brosilla Lamin of Mawlai, who was Mawlong's colleague in the District Council. Eventually, they felt convinced that he was a suitable match for her. In 1977, Ria shifted from Umïam to Delina's House at Lower Mawprem. It was in Delina's house that Mawlong formally asked for Ria's hand. It was a simple and straight-forward proposal, which Ria's guardians readily agreed to.

Unlike these days where MLAs and MDCs move around in swanky SUVs, Mawlong himself an MDC like other of his colleagues, had meagre resources. So it took time to make satisfactory marital arrangements. Their wedding was a simple but memorable affair on 14 May 1978 at Mawlai Catholic Church. Ria was dressed in a modest yet graceful gown and the rituals were completed in the presence of a few relatives.

The newlyweds at first stayed in the same rented house at Mission Compound. They shifted to a bigger rented house at Lumsohphoh in Lower Mawprem after the birth of their first child, George Bankyntiewlang Lyngdoh Mawphlang. Mawlong's nieces, Eloris and Erimai fondly called Mem and Bih, continued to stay with them, as by that time they had become like his own children. The two continued to pursue their studies and simultaneously helped out at home, and gained much affection from the infant George and subsequently that of his siblings one to four years apart, Wandashisha, Damaphishisha, Andrew

Wanbanjoplang, Ferdinand Banshanlang, the author of this book, and John Hubert Banraplang. After Eloris completed her studies, she left for the village as she was the only daughter and had to take care of her ailing mother. She later took up a teaching job but Erimai continued to stay on.

In his frequent visits to Umroi, Mawlong befriended Tholen Marbaniang and Josila Thangkhiew of Lumshyiap village. As Josila was of the Thangkhiew clan, Mawlong addressed her as *Kha,*[95] as Mawlong's father was also a Thangkhiew. In his visits to their house, he observed their struggles and poverty. Just as Babu Sosto Manik Syiem and Helen Giri's family took him under their wing in his school days, he volunteered to be the benefactor for two of their ten children, Persia and Berlasting Thangkhiew. The siblings too stayed with his family till they completed their studies in the late 1980s.

Their rented house at Lower Mawprem was never free of visitors except when Mawlong was away on tour. KM Warjri, his former student who later became a close aide, recalled how the landowners provided a separate cooking space to cater to the large number of visitors seeking Mawlong's assistance on a number of problems. There were times when Warjri felt people took undue advantage of Mawlong and often cautioned

95 Paternal aunt

him but he never agreed. No matter how unhygienic or untidy the villagers appeared, to Mawlong, they were equal as he was elected to look after them and their welfare. But Warjri felt that he was too giving and trusted people very easily. Apart from raising their six children, Mawlong and Ria were also taking care of educating the foster ones, and unremittingly meeting innumerable people every day.

In February 1983, a proposal was made by Winstone Syiemïong and SD Khongwir to Mawlong to move to a bigger house, the official bungalow of the Speaker, as they were unanimous in their decision to get him elected when the regional parties–HPU, HSPDP, and PDIC–came together to form the Meghalaya United Parliamentary Party (MUPP) Government. A hesitant Ria inquired from Khongwir what would happen to them if Mawlong, who then belonged to the HSPDP, was dislodged from the chair. She was naturally worried about their stay if asked to vacate the bungalow. A confident Khongwir assured her that their Government would last for the entire five years and she needn't be worried. After Mawlong's election as Speaker in March 1983, the family shifted to Lake House, the official residence of the Speaker of the Legislative Assembly.

However, the Government collapsed after twenty-five days. The Congress yet again came into power and the HSPDP was pushed to the

Opposition bench. There was uncertainty whether they'd be able to continue staying in the Lake House. And if they had to vacate, they'd have to rent a new place. However, an undeterred Mawlong calmly reiterated to his wife that impeaching the Speaker was not easy. As long as he exercised impartiality, there was no reason for the members of the Assembly to remove him. He continued to be Speaker till the end of the term in 1987-88.

The days spent in Lake House were memorable. They, however, occupied the official residence only till 1986. Their permanent residence at Lumsohphoh, Lower Mawprem, whose construction started in 1983, was partially complete. They shifted to the newly built house amidst support from friendly neighbours as the rented house they stayed in earlier was in the same locality.

The Mawlong household was always a busy one. People from all walks of life would make a beeline from the early hours, notwithstanding the day of the week. There was no fixed time for visits like the ones in a doctor's clinic. Depending upon the urgency, people's visits were often sudden and unexpected. Due to the limited facilities available in their villages right from the 1970s up to the 1990s, most villagers had to travel to Shillong, particularly to nurse the infirm. Like most public figures of the day, Mawlong had to deal with the twin purposes of developing the constituency and meeting personal requirements of the people. There were times when

family members would complain about the lack of quality family time but if anyone admonished the visitors, mostly modest farmers who possessed the bare minimum of life's requirements, they would have to endure his disapproval. Visitors were never turned away without a cup of tea or the customary *kwai.*[96] Some weekends were reserved for meetings at his residence to chalk out details of various schemes where party workers from Umroi and headmen of various villages would converge. Once in five years, the election season saw the footfall of many ardent supporters.

Due to such commitments to the public, family outings were often cancelled at the last moment as Mawlong would be caught up in some programme or busy attending meetings. But his work wasn't above everything else, as whatever task he took up, he remained adequately involved in it. Ria recalls that no matter how busy he was, if he had access to a telephone, he always made it a habit to call home at least once a day to inquire about the children. He always accompanied them when parents were called to receive the mid-year and annual progress reports in school. He also made it a point to take his children to Umroi on weekends to watch football matches or visit different villages. The proximity of his children towards the people was imminent but he never thrust them too much into the limelight,

96 Betel nut eaten together with betel leaf and a dash of lime

and didn't encourage them to be too involved in his work. He would overtly express that education was the most important thing. If the children wished to follow in his footsteps, they would have to be educated and capable enough, he would say.

A politician's time is never his own and the enormous work involved can never be managed single-handedly. For most of the thirty years that he was in public service, there were many acquaintances and friends who helped him. Biwot Lanong was one such individual who remained faithful to Mawlong and his family. In the 1980s and early 1990s, when movies could be viewed in cinema halls or privately at home using a Video Cassette Recorder (VCR), the people of the villages in Umroi constituency always looked forward to the winter season. After they harvested paddy and the festive season of Christmas and annual community feasts beckoned, Mawlong would send Lanong together with KM Warjri or his brother-in-law, Ronnie Lyngdoh along with a television, a VCR, a collection of Hindi movies, and a generator in his faithful Ambassador car. The movies, particularly Mithun Chakraborty's *Dance Dance* and *Disco Dancer*, enthralled the people and they revelled to the music of Bappi Lahiri. The news that such shows were held in Umroi spread to other villages in Sohïong constituency. The same drill had to be repeated on a few occasions in his home village Mawmih and adjoining villages owing to popular demand.

Since his formative years, Mawlong was inclined towards reading and writing, particularly journalistic writing. In 1989, the owners of *U Nongsaiñ Hima*, a Khasi vernacular newspaper, were in search for potential buyers as they could no longer manage the newspaper. The paper was first published in December 1960, during the commencement of the Hill State movement to demand for a separate state, and its founder was Prof George Gilbert Swell, a former Member of Parliament. Si Sohtun, an acquaintance and staff of George Hamilton, the Editor of the paper who had recently passed away, visited Mawlong at his residence and wondered if he was interested. Hamilton also owned a printing press called The Modern Printing Press and a letterpress, located at the premises of the Khasi National Durbar Hall at Mawkhar. Si Sohtun offered both, the rights to publish the paper and the letterpress to Mawlong. The eager Mawlong reasoned with his wife that the letterpress and the newspaper business could be a profitable venture provided they could get dedicated staff. And if they could sustain it, his children could look after it in future when they'd come of age. Though the asking price was beyond his means, he availed a loan of Rs 50,000 from a public sector bank, and made the paper and the press his own. The first among a few staff he recruited was Biwot Lanong, having observed his sincerity and integrity in any task that was assigned

to him. Lanong first did odd jobs in the letterpress and after being trained by Sohtun, helped in the printing of notices, pamphlets, posters, and other jobwork. Later, he oversaw the circulation of the newspaper and also helped the reporters whenever he could. The paper was first published as a weekly, remaining so till the year 1990; then it was made into a bi-weekly, and subsequently to a daily in the year 1992. As the letterpress could only cater to printing pamphlets, posters and notices, the newspaper had to be printed in Agardoot Press located in distant Guwahati. Later, it was printed in Ri Khasi Press and subsequently in the Offset Press of *The Shillong Times*, the oldest English daily of the state. Ria had a big hand in sustaining the paper and remained actively involved from 1989 till the year 2006. She was also trained by Sohtun on how to manage the printing business and devoted much of her time there during the day. In the evening and late into the night, she'd prepare meals for all the reporters and typists who were working in the newspaper and stayed up till the work was completed which was usually past midnight. By five in the morning, she'd dash to Motphran (Ïewduh) to hand over the newspapers to vendors and hawkers.

The newspaper was indeed very popular in the 1990s but suffered a major slump from the year 2000 to 2004. Its circulation went down drastically and it was on the verge of being shut

down. As they didn't have an offset machine of their own and had to print in *The Shillong Times,* it was becoming increasingly difficult to sustain. In 2005, Mawlong had to again make another decision pertaining to the paper. Surrounded by his closest aides including Syndor Sing Syiem and Lambok Thabah, both associated with the paper as former editor and incumbent editor respectively, they felt that closing down the paper would amount to a missed opportunity. In the end, they unanimously decided to take a calculated risk. Mawlong availed another loan to purchase an offset printing machine. His eldest son George, an engineering graduate, was instrumental in reviving the paper. He took an active part in the overall management of the paper including enhancing the advertisement revenue, and increasing the circulation of the paper. Fortunately, the risk paid off and *U Nongsaiñ Hima* was once again popular in the Khasi-Jaiñtia Hills. And just as he had envisioned, four of his children—George, Damaphishisha, Andrew, and John are now actively involved in the day-to-day affairs of the paper.

Most of the decisions Mawlong took in his political career had an impact on his near ones. In December 1999, during the Chief Ministership of BB Lyngdoh, some MLAs from the United Democratic Party (UDP) and the coalition partners in the Government started garnering support to make Mawlong the next Chief Minister. When he confided this to his wife, she dissuaded him from

taking such a step. She reasoned that if looking after a single constituency required so much time and effort; manning the entire state was going to be an enormous task. She had already witnessed the political uncertainty that befell the fate of past governments. Coalition politics was a tough task and she feared that Mawlong, who trusted people easily, could be falling into a political trap. She told him that good or bad, the family would eventually face the brunt. Since the post of Speaker, which he held at that time was the most dignified post, remaining in it would bode well for everyone. But Mawlong wasn't persuaded. He reasoned that some disgruntled MLAs were ready to leave the party to join hands with others. The UDP, which was formed after so much effort, would disintegrate and he couldn't let that happen.

On 8 March 2000, the day Mawlong was sworn in as Chief Minister, was a joyous event for family and friends. Acquaintances from near and far visited a day earlier to the ceremony. The endless stream of visitors continued for many days after that. The house at Lower Mawprem could no longer hold the visitors so, it was suggested that the family should shift to the Chief Minister's official residence, the Tara Ghar Bungalow opposite the picturesque Ward's Lake, a popular tourist destination. According to Khasi belief, it is inauspicious to carry out a new endeavour in April. Hence, they shifted in March itself.

The eighteen months that he was Chief Minister were indeed a hectic time for Mawlong as he was constantly travelling, attending endless meetings, and most of all, was in the public gaze more than before. An unconducive law and order situation owing to heightened militant activities in the state, agitations by pressure groups, and the fragile political situation compounded the work pressure upon Mawlong. Already hypertensive and diabetic for many years, he began to make a conscious effort to manage his health.

Then there was the *Ksan Rngiew Movement*, an agitation propelled by the Khasi Students' Union (KSU) to pressurise the Government to change the reservation policy, in place since 1972, which reserves 40 per cent of Government jobs for the Khasi and Jaiñtia, 40 per cent for the Garos, and 20 per cent for the other tribes and general categories. The KSU's demand to increase the share of the Khasis and Jaiñtias saw an unprecedented participation of school and college students. Suspected members of the Union allegedly stoned Mawlong's house at Lower Mawprem. In the cover of night, hand-sized stones were hurled towards the frontage of the house leaving behind a mess of shards. The event led to the unpalatable realisation that the agitation had turned personal. He conveyed his bafflement over the aggressiveness shown by the Union because the matter pertaining to the change in the job reservation was unviable. The

Nationalist Congress Party (NCP), a major partner in the Government, comprised mostly of Garo legislators. The same was the case in the Congress party. The MLAs of the United Democratic Party (UDP) were mostly from the Khasi-Jaiñtia region, but numbers were insufficient to bring about an amendment in the policy. His sagacious decision to constitute a committee to look into the matter did silence the agitators for a while.

Another agitation that erupted on the streets of Shillong against the controversial Kolkata Meghalaya House Deal led by the People's Rally Against Corruption (PRAC) was perhaps the most unpleasant experience that had a long-lasting detrimental effect on him and his family. False allegations of corruption were levelled against him, his cabinet colleague Nimarson Momin, and senior officers of the Government. The relentless public outcry over the alleged 'sell-out' of the Meghalaya House led to the Government cancelling the deal and instituting a judicial inquiry, thereby, fulfilling the demands of the agitators. But the group kept pressing for his resignation as they alleged that he had indulged in corruption. The political situation soon turned fluid, with detractors within his Government and those in the opposition trying their best to unseat him. The UDP's ally, the Nationalist Congress Party (NCP), played truant and finally pulled out of the Government. Seven UDP legislators–BB Lyngdoh, AH Scott Lyngdoh,

Martle Mukhim, DP Iangjuh, Simon Siangshai, PT Sawkmie and Rasor Rani–broke away from the party to form the Meghalaya United Democratic Party (MUDP). He was most dismayed that his close friend and General Secretary of the NCP, Purno A Sangma refused to take his calls or even meet him during the course of the political instability. From then on, the relation between the two was under duress. They never reconciled.

On 7 December 2001, when a No-Confidence Motion was discussed in the Assembly, he was dismayed that the Speaker, Elstone D Marak, didn't allow him to clarify his stance. The 'political ploy' as he called it, was near its end but he was relatively content as during his time the ginger farmers fetched a profitable price for their produce, contractors' bills were cleared timely, teachers were paid on time, and many pending projects saw the light of day. Though people were within their rights to agitate, he felt that the personal attacks were unwarranted as there was no substantial proof against him having underhand dealings. No head of Government, according to him, faced so much of public scrutiny and ill-will.

The split in the UDP saddened him, with many pointing fingers that his delay in taking a resolute decision pertaining to the Meghalaya House deal, and his unwillingness to resign as Chief Minister, led to its downfall. However, he felt that resigning at that time would have been

equivalent to conceding guilt, and reaffirmed that he didn't indulge in any wrongdoing. In 1989, he bought a second-hand Ambassador car and a jeep, and after many years, bought a paddy field at Nongpyrdet village. Nobody could prove he gained disproportionate wealth, he would reason. He reiterated that it was due to the indiscipline of the MLAs and the ambition of some colleagues who wanted to replace him that led to the split in the UDP. He resigned on 8 December 2001. By then, his health had deteriorated drastically.

On the day of his resignation, there was an unusual silence around Tara Ghar. Being indisposed, he was confined to his room, and the daily stream of visitors had dried up. The next Government was sworn in with Dr Flinder Anderson Khonglam, an independent legislator, as Chief Minister. A few days thereafter, accompanied by his wife Ria, her cousin Dr Ermelinda Lyngdoh, and family friend Dr Andreas Dkhar, he left for Chennai for further treatment and returned after almost two months in February 2002, exactly a year before the next General Election. After his return, the remaining UDP legislators met at his private residence. They wanted him as president of the party to negotiate with NCP and the Congress to induct the UDP in the new Government. Most of them were of the opinion that being in the Opposition would not augur well, and he ought to be in power to do well in the election. He reasoned that the move might

backfire and the public would lose faith in the party and his leadership. But the headstrong MLAs felt otherwise. Left with no alternative, he met Purno A Sangma, for a one-to-one, and some UDP legislators were inducted into the Khonglam ministry.

After his return from Chennai and a few months' rest, he sought to win back the confidence of the people. As President of the UDP, he extensively toured various places in the months leading to the election. In the constituencies where the party was weakened due the desertion of the seven MLAs, the party found replacements. It became obvious that he wanted to recreate the magic of the UDP like in 1998. In most of the meetings, he refuted the allegations against him and his Government, and welcomed a probe by any agency to ascertain the truth. But few noticed his state of mind. Only those close to him like his nephew Rijan Mawlong, noticed that there was a distinct change in his ways in the runup to the elections. Rijan says that Mawlong was quite cantankerous and lost patience quickly in contrast to his earlier days.

In his home constituency Umroi, Stanlywiss Rymbai of the Congress party was his only opponent, making it a one-on-one contest. Babu Dwikshon Kharkongor recalls that Mawlong visited the constituency only twice in the two months leading to the election. He appeared only in the rally at Umroi and Mawlasnai villages. Anti-incumbency was also at a high considering the lack of clarity in

the people's minds over the events that occurred during his Chief Ministership. Eventually when votes were counted on 1 March 2003, he lost to Rymbai by 1,093 votes. The UDP won a mere nine seats from the twenty that it had wrested in 1998. The unexpected loss in the election and an unclear stand over the allegations left him and his family in a precarious position. None of the children were employed yet and he was the only bread earner. His newspaper, *U Nongsaiñ Hima*, was also not doing well. It was indeed an uncertain period.

A multi-party Government led by the Congress was sworn in after the election. DD Lapang was elected as leader of the Congress Legislature Party and took over as Chief Minister. The nine UDP MLAs also joined the Government and most were made Ministers or Chairmen of various boards and commissions. Mawlong was given the post of Co-Chairman of the State Development Reforms Commission alongside veteran Congress leader Dhruba Nath Joshi.

The adjustment period after his loss was a difficult time and his supporters and well-wishers visited him often. He spent his mornings in their company and in the afternoons, he whiled away his time in front of the television or reading the newspapers and books. He followed the news on television and keenly watched the debates in Lok Sabha and Rajya Sabha. As four of his children were based in Shillong pursuing studies, he was able

to spend quality time with them in the evening, regularly praying together.

Sometime in August 2003 after the passing away of sitting legislator from Laban, TH Rangad, the restless Mawlong was briefly taken in by the willingness shown by a few people of Laban who encouraged him to contest the impending bye-election. He did show his eagerness and was indeed tempted by the prospect of returning to state politics. But a few close friends like the Parish Priest of Laban Parish, Fr John Madur, dissuaded him, considering that late Rangad's wife was the BJP candidate and the sympathy wave would definitely favour her. The BJP candidate won the bye-election very convincingly. Thereafter, he spent most of his days at home, often visiting Umroi to meet his supporters.

The singular thing that bothered him in those years was the blot on his image owing to the corruption allegations over the Meghalaya House deal. He wanted to clear his name of all allegations. In 2005, the passage of the Right to Information Act (RTI) accorded him an opportunity to find out the status of the case. The SP Rajkhowa Judicial Inquiry Commission instituted by the FA Khonglam Government was disbanded and it didn't submit any report as there were allegations that Rajkhowa was biased. Also, most of the pressure group leaders who had made the allegations against Mawlong didn't depose before the commission.

The Government had decided to hand over the case to the Central Bureau of Investigation (CBI) to ascertain if there was indeed any wrongdoing or financial irregularity. However, almost five years after that the matter remained dormant. Frustrated, Mawlong decided to seek information from the Government under the RTI but the reply he received indicated that there was no progress at all in the case. The Government had sought the CBI's intervention but the latter asked for the Inquiry Report of the Rajkhowa Commission before it could proceed. Irked by the slackness, he decided to file a petition in the Shillong Bench of the Guwahati High Court. Taking the views of his wife and his children, he went ahead and filed a Writ Petition after a detailed discussion with his lawyer, MJ Ahmed.

A favourable verdict from the Honourable High Court owing to a lack of 'prima facie evidence' vindicated his stand, much to his relief. The court in its verdict stated that like all human beings he should be 'let alone to enjoy life without fetters.' It further stated that 'the sweeping power of investigation does not warrant subjecting a citizen to investigation, harassment, mental agony and a loss of reputation.' The corruption allegations were indeed a great loss of reputation and peace of mind not only for Mawlong but the entire family. For much of the uncertain years before the court cleared his name, he didn't socialise much and avoided

attending large public functions and gatherings. The day of the verdict on 10 January2008 was indeed a memorable day. The following day, the judgement made it to the screaming headlines of the local dailies. The impending Assembly election was in two months' time, thus the verdict's timing was indeed favourable. Mawlong was ready to fight another election from Umroi on a UDP ticket.

Jovial as he was, supporters recall a comical incident that happened during the runup to his last election. His house as usual was full of people from Umroi, and in attendance was a senior party worker, who was known for his promiscuous ways. Children from the locality would run around in the compound, some jumping on the chance to request for a UDP flag, so they could wave it around to join the election frenzy. The party worker noticed two children who were continuously persisting for some flags. As he had a bundle of the red, white, and green UDP flags, he gave each one a piece, and told them to shake Mawlong's hand as a token of thanks, and to wish him luck. Mawlong was seated on a chair in the drawing room talking to some people, and the party worker thrusted the two kids towards him. Mawlong readily shook their little hands, but questioned:

'Who are these kids?'

'I don't know them, Ma Heh, they wanted some flags so I gave them two,' replied the promiscuous party worker.

Mawlong's witty reply evoked a hearty laugh: 'So, do you know the mother?'

Despite his determination, five years of little activity and dependence on medicines had weakened him to a considerable extent. There were days when he was down with flu for long periods. As the election approached, there was little improvement in his health. During the campaign period, he couldn't attend meetings and other partymen had to make up for his absence. One day while sick in bed, he called his eldest son, George, for a quiet word. He told him that he no longer had the same strength to travel to the villages to campaign for the election though his spirit was ever willing. He told George to take the lead in the campaign and work together with the leaders. Whenever he could, he would attend meetings. Nervous, the eldest son shed tears of agony but didn't want to disappoint his ailing father. The thirty-one-year-old showed maturity and led the campaign from the front.

Mawlong couldn't attend a single meeting leading up to voting day, except at the last rally at Umroi Nongrah where he could speak for less than five minutes. Most of the people in the large crowd had tears in their eyes on seeing their ailing leader whose appearance had changed considerably. The vote count on 7 March 2008 showed that Mawlong had defeated six other candidates, surpassing his nearest rival, Stanlywiss Rymbai, by 926 votes. It was indeed a miraculous win. Having been in the

company of villagers and supporters throughout his adult life, the five-year break from politics was indeed agonising days, and everyone felt that his comeback would strengthen his spirit.

The UDP won eleven seats in all and supported a Government led by the NCP. After a brief recovery in April, he invited some members of the cabinet to visit Umroi for an interaction with the people and to know their aspirations. That was to be his last participation in a public meeting. On 8 August, after another spell of kidney-related illness, he was taken to Civil Hospital in an unconscious state. He regained consciousness after a few days and slowly recovered to almost normalcy.

After two months and five days in the hospital, one evening he suddenly grew restless and expressed his desire to return home. Notwithstanding the advice of doctors and relatives, he was adamant about being discharged. On the evening of 15 October, as he was driven home, he didn't speak much during the short drive. He had his meal and smiled warmly at everyone who was around him. The next morning, he again took ill and returned to the same hospital room which he had vacated the day before. Subsequently, he slipped into unconsciousness and passed away on the morning of 17 October.

The incumbent Chief Minister, Dr Donkupar Roy of the UDP and Minister John Anthony Lyngdoh were among the first to arrive at the

hospital. The Government's offer to conduct a state funeral in his honour was turned down by the family as they wished to have a simple ceremony, symbolic of his simple lifestyle. A requiem mass was offered by the Archbishop of Shillong Archdiocese, Dominic Jala, and rich tributes were paid by Government functionaries and friends. He was laid to rest at Mawprem Catholic Cemetery and as the coffin was carted up the steep road towards his final resting place, a huge multitude followed closely behind.

He lived surrounded by the masses whom he loved, and finally rested in the presence of thousands of people.

In Remembrance

DONGMUSA

VOL.II NO.8 Regd. No. 40819/84 SNGITHOHDIENG 7 RYMPHANG 1986 SHI TYNGKA

Shen yn kylla myntri ha jylla

SHILLONG: Katkum ki khubor ba la paw, shen kan don ka jingpynkylla ia ki myntri ka sorkar jylla ha Shillong khnang ban pynlong ia ka sorkar kaba ia jan bad batrei na ka bynta ki paidbah. Kane ka jingpynkylla ka ban wan: ka la paw na ki katto katne ki rangbah Congress (I) kiba iathuh ba u Capt. W.A. Sangma u thrang bad u angnud ban iai trei shitom na ka bynta ka jingroi jingpa ki paidbah.

U A.K. Anthony, general secretary AICC(I) u la pynlyngkot ia ka jingleit jngoh jong u ia ka Manipur bad u la wanher bak bak sha Shillong.

Napdeng ki myntri ka sorkar jylla, mynta ka don ka jinglynga jingpisa bad jingkyan mynsiem ioh ki duh noh ia ki shuki synshar. Hapdeng kito kiba dang iai ap khmih lynti ia ki shuki synshar ki dang iai jaw syep bad pisa mynsiem ban iohsngew noh kloi ba ki kyrteng jong ki ruh kin paw bad mih pyrthei.

Katkum ki khubor na ki dkhot ka seng Congress (I) la don ka jingsuba ba u Myntri Rangbah ka jylla Capt. W.A. Sangma u lah ban sloit noh katto katne ngut na ki nyntri bamynta bad u lah ruh ban pynrung ia kiwei pat kibathymmai ha ka kynhun ka ban dang mih shen. Ki iathuh ruh ba don ka jingsyier hapdeng ki myntri cabinet ba yn don ka jingpynkylla ia ki katto katne ngut bad ha ki jaka jong ki yn ai noh ha kiwei pat.

U A.K. Anthony u la iakren bniah bha bad u Myntri Rangbah Capt. W.A. Sangma halor ki kam pynthymmai ia ki rukom trei kam ka seng bad ban jied ia ki nongkitkam ka seng da kiwei pat kiba kham pyngngad jabieng, khnang ban kham lah ban trei satar na ka bnynta ka seng ha kine ki khyndiat snem.

Trei ka khun ia ka kmie

PADU: Ka khubor ba la poi slem na Padu, ka shnong kaba jngai kumba 32 Km na Jowai sha lynti Dawki, ha kaba ka khun kaba kyrteng ka Rani Mukhim ka la pom lyngkhot lyngkhai ia la ka kmie kaba kyrteng ka Pdok Mukhim da ka wait ngor dieng.

Kane ka jing jia batreim ka la jia ha ka por janmiet ha ka 13 tarik u Kyllalyngkot hakaba ka khun ka la pom ia la ka kmie na ka jingiaka jia ba ka kmie kam ju ai pisa ia ka kane ka khun, hynrei ka theh spah tang sha u khun shynrang jong ka.

La ong ba ka kmie ka la shah pom lyngkhot lyngkhai naduh kjat haduh khlieh ha ka khun jong ka. Haba pulit ki la rah ia ka kmie sha hospital kawei ka kjat jong ka ka la hap ha madan ka jing jylliew ka jingpom kata ka khun. Ka kmie ka la iap ha lynti.

La pdiang sngewbha ia u kpa Bekhuid Pope John Paul II da u Myntri Rangbah Capt. W.A Sangma, u Lat ka jylla B.N. Singh, u Shongknor ka iingdorbar Thawain ka jylla Bah E.K. Mawlong ha Shillong Helipad ha ka step 4 tarik mynta u bnai. Dongmusa Photo

Pynneh ki dustur nylla: Pope John

SHILLONG: Ka sor Shillong ha ka 4 tarik mynta u bnai ka la riam la beit da ki rong ki rup baitynnat ban pdiang burom ia u Pope John Paul II, u Khliehduh jong ki 850 millian ngut ki paid Katholik satlak ka pyrthei. U Pope u la iuhkjat ha jaka hiar helikopter ha Umdiengpun ha ka por 9.40 mynstep bad la pdiang burom ia u da u Lat ka jylla B.N. Singh, Myntri Rangbah Capt. W.A. Sangma, Shongknor ka Iingdorbar Thawain ka jylla Bah. E.K. Mawlong, ryngkat bad ki phra ngut ki bishop na kane ka thain ba la lamkhmat da u Rev. Archbishop Hubert D'Rosario, ka jylla-niam Shillong-Guwahati.

Mar ia hiar na helikopter, u Pope u la pynpaw ka jingsngewkmen da kaba ong: "ka mynsiem jong nga ka shlei da ka jingkmen ban wan sha kine ki lum baitynnat jong kane ka thain."

Na Umdiengpun la ialam beit beit ia u Pope sha madan Golf Link ha kaba ki paidbah babun ki la ap khmih lynti ia u. La pdiangburom ia u Pope da iwei i khynnah kynthei khunswet iba la pyndeng syntiew ia ka ryndang jong u Kpa Bakhuid, uba la pynphai kylliang ia ka jingieid bad jingsngewburom jong u da kaba doh kylla ia i.

U Pope u la pynmynta ia ka jingknia Mass ha kaba la shim bynta lang da ki Kardinal, ki Bishop, ki phadar hakhmat ki 2 lak tam ki paidbah kiba la pyndap bad pynphuh ia ka madan da ki riam ki beit babun rong.

Ha ka jingkren paidbah u Pope u la iaroh ia ka jingtynnat jong ki riti ki dustur jong ki jaitbynriew bashong basah ha kane ka thain. "Kane" u ong "ka pynkynmaw ia ka jingdap jong u Blei da ka jingisynei." U la kren iaroh ruh ia ka jingiajan jong u Blei bad u briew ha kane ka thain kaba pyni shynna ia ki matti babha jong u Blei lyngba ki jinglong jingman baluilui ba ki paid nongshongshnong kane ka thain ki iai im sngi ha la ki kam ki jam bad ha la ki jinglong, hynrei U im U sah ryngkat bad phi," la ong u nongsyn-shar mynsiem. U kdew ruh ba ka mariang, bad ki jingitynnat jong ka, ki iai pasiaw ia ki jinglong bamaian u Blei ha kane ka thain.

U Pope u la iaroh ruh ia ki jingtrei shitom bad jingpha jong ki nongtrei mynsiem kiba la wan ha kane ka thain ha ki spah snem ba la dep. U la niew tang ia ka umsyep ba la theh da u Phadar Krick bad Phadar Boury kiba la wanrah nyngkong ia ka jingshai jong ka jingpynim. U la kren iaroh ruh ia ki jingtrei shitom jong kiwei pat ki Balang Khristan bym dei Katholik ha ka jingpynphriang ia ka ktien jong u Blei ha ki jaitbynriew bapher bapher jong kane ka thain. "Ia kine baroh ngi dap da ka jingkynmaw ieid bad jingsngewnguh, kiba la bet ia u symbai ka jingshai ka Ktien u Blei lyngba ki jingeh bym lah niewtang," u la ong.

U la pynkynmaw ia ki paidbah ba ka jingshai Khristan ka wan ym ban iuhroit ia ki jinglongtynrai, ki dustur ki riti bad ki jingsngew jan para briew, "hynrei ka jingshai Khristan ka dei ban pdiang bad pynjanai ia kine ki sap bakyrpang ba kawei pa kawei ka jaitbynriew ka don." U la ban ktien ruh da kaba ong, "Kine ki dustur ki riti ba ki kynhun jaitbynriew bapher bapher ha kane ka thain ki don, ki dei ban pynphuh pynphieng ia ka Balang, namar ia ki la ri bad la sumar kyndong naduh ki por bym lah wad dien trai."

U Pope u tynrong lem ruh ia ki jingeh ba kane ka juk mynta ka iakynduh kumba shem lem kiwei pat ki jaka ha ka pyrthei. Da ka mynsiem basngewthuh bad sngewsynei u ong ba ki jingeh, ki jinglynga mynsiem bad ki jingduk jingkyrduh ba kynrei ha kane ka por ki long ki jingeh ba ka pyrthei hi baroh kawei ka shem. "Ki dawai ia kine ki jingeh yn nym lah shem satia ha ki jinghikai kiba don ha ki rukom pyrkhat ha la ki riti ki dustur. Hynrei ia ki dawai pynkoit lah ban shem tang ha ki jingthoh ha ka Ktien u Blei, kaba pyni shynna ia ka jingieid bamaian jong u Blei ia ngi ki briew. Dei u Krist Uba long shisha u nongpynbiang ia ki jingangnud jong ki jaitbynriew baroh," u ong.

U Pope u kyntu ia ki nongtrei ha ktien u Blei ba ki dei ban pynphuh pynphieng ia ka Balang da kaba bynrap da ki jingitynnat jong ka jinglong batynrai ba ki jaitbynriew ki don.

U kyntu ia ki nongtrei Balang baroh ba kin iai tylli mlon kawei ka jingmut jingpyrkhat ha ki kam pynphriang ia ka ktien u Blei.

U kren kyrpang ia ki samla kane ka thain da kaba pynshlur ia ki ban ieid bad ban sumar kyndong ia la ki dustur ki riti, ka ktien ka thylliej bad ia ki histori jong ka jaitynriew.

U ong ruh ba ha ka tyrpeng jong ki samla ia ka khubor babha jong ka jingpynim ka shonglyngngeit ban pynphriang shaduh bakut jong kane ka thain Lam Mihngi ka ri India.

U Rev. Archbishop ka Shillong-Guwahati Hubert D'Rosario u la kren pdiang burom ia u Pope John Paul II habasdang ka jinglehniam. U ong ba ki paidbah jong kane ka thain ki iaikhmih lynti ia kane ka sngi da ka jingkmen bad jingduwai mynsiem.

U Pope John Paul II u la pynkut ia ka jinglehniam da kaba khublei ia ki paidbah ha ka ktien Khasi.

"KHUBLEI U BLEI UN KYRKHU IA PHI BAROH!"

Ha ka por jinglehniam la wanrah ruh ia ki 16 hynriew tylli ki jingshad bapher na ki jylla bapher bapher kane ka thain, kiba pyni ba ki long shibynta na ka jinglehniam lehrukom. U Pope u la sam kommunion ha ki 36 ngut kiba pang bashitom ka met kiba na kane ka thain.

Mar iadep ki jinglehniam, u Pope u la leit beit sha Umdiengpun ban leit phai noh sha Calcutta. U la kiew ha ka helikopter shipai ha ka por 1.20 nohphai sngi.

U Pope u la kren iaroh ruh ia ka sorkar Meghalaya kaba la leh shitom ban pynkhreh bad ban pdiang burom ia u ha ka jingwan jngoh ia ka sor Shillong.

A clipping from the vernacular *Dongmusa* where EK Mawlong, Capt Williamson A Sangma greet Pope John Paul II after he landed at Upper Shillong during his visit in 1986.

At a programme organised by St Anthony's School, Shillong.

At Dal Lake.

At his last election rally at Umroi in 2008.

At the Meghalaya Legislative Assembly premises.

Commissioning of the Regulated Market at Mawiong in September 2001.

Enjoying a pony ride in Srinagar.

His hearty self on a conference in Srinagar.

On May 16, 1979, his wedding day.

On one of his birthdays.

Receiving the Manav Sewa Puraskar in 1998 from Former Governor of Meghalaya, Bhisma Narayan Singh.

Sharing a light moment with Farooq Abdullah.

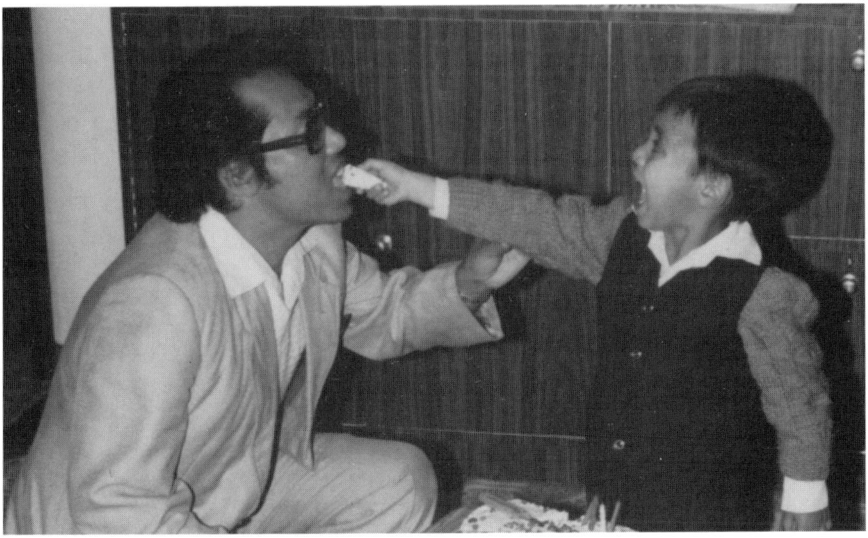

The Family Man.

With Atal Bihari Bajpayee and PK Mahanta.

With Dr DD Lapang, JD Rymbai and other dignitaries during the inauguration of Jirang C&RD Block.

With Emerson Thangkhiew (grey suit) and other family members during a memorial service of Yiem Mawlong, his mother, at Mawmih village.

With family and Archbishop Hubert D' Rosario.

With Former Chief Minister of Assam, Tarun Gogoi.

With Former MP PR Kyndiah.

With Governor MM Jacob during the inauguration of the Umrynjah Bridge.

With leaders LK Advani and Zoramthanga.

Bejewelled in traditional finery, EK Mawlong at the State Central Library, Shillong, premises after his vectory in the 1972 MDC election from Umroi.

With PA Sangma at his home at Lower Mawprem.

With PK Mahanta, CM of Assam during a visit to Maikhuli.

With Rajiv Gandhi during the SAARC Summit in Shillong, 1985.

Certificates from various phases of life

IIFS

BHARAT JYOTI AWARD

Certificate Of Excellence

Presented to

Late Shri E K Mawlong

For Meritorious Services, Outstanding Performance And Remarkable Role

By

Mr. A Rajbansi, MPL

(MEC for Sport & Recreation) KwaZulu Natal

Govt. of South Africa

NETAJI BIRTHDAY CELEBRATION COMMITTEE

10, WATERLOO STREET, KOLKATA - 700 069
Regd. No. S/71696

CERTIFICATE OF FELICITATION

This is to certify that

Shri E. K. Mawlong (Hon'ble Chief Minister of Meghalaya)

is hereby awarded

NETAJI AWARD, 2000

for his outstanding contribution in the field of National Amity and Co-operation

On 4th November, 2000, at Kala Kunj, Calcutta

NATIONAL CITIZEN'S AWARD

PRESENTED BY

MR. JUSTICE P. N. BHAGWATI

HON'BLE CHAIRMAN, UNITED NATIONS HUMAN RIGHTS' COMMITTEE

TO

MR. E. K. MAWLONG

CHIEF MINISTER OF MEGHALAYA

FOR HIS REMARKABLE SUCCESS IN SECURING PEACE, PROGRESS AND DEVELOPMENT IN MEGHALAYA

ON AUGUST 25, 2001 AT NEW DELHI

JURY :

MR. JUSTICE P.N. BHAGWATI
MR. HIPHEI, MP
DR. FAROOQ ABDULLAH
MR. V. NARAYANASAMY, EX. MP
MR. S.C. JAMIR
MR. SATCHIDANANDA
MR. SYED SHAH NAWAZ HUSSAIN
RAJA VIJAY KARAN, IPS